# JIM FISK

# CLEMATIS

## THE QUEEN OF CLIMBERS

CASSELL

Cassell Publishers Limited
Artillery House, Artillery Row
London SW1P 1RT

First published in this edition 1989

**British Library Cataloguing in Publication Data**
Fisk, Jim
   Clematis — the queen of climbers — 3rd ed.
   1. Gardens. Clematis
   I. [The Queen of Climbers] II. Title
   635.9'33111

ISBN  0  304  31620  2

Filmset by Bestset Typesetters Ltd, Hong Kong

Printed in Portugal by Printer Portuguesa Industria Grafica Lda.

*Frontispiece: C. texenis* 'Gravetye Beauty', 'Henyri' and 'Perle
d'Azur' scrambling over an archway in a Yorkshire garden.

# CONTENTS

# ACKNOWLEDGEMENTS

To those friends who so kindly supplied photographs of their clematis for this book, I express my most grateful thanks. To those whose photographs were not finally chosen, I can only offer my apologies, and the explanation that it was very difficult to make the selection from the many excellent ones I received. A very big 'thank you' to you all for your photographs and your help: —

G. E. Barrett; Freida Brown; Peter Cox; Terence E. Exley; Keith Fair; John Fopma; S. I. Francis; Stefan Franczak; Ken Gardner; Bridget Gubbins; Jennifer Hewitt; A. Horsfall; D. G. Hunt; Thelma Kay; Alister Keay; Tony Lord; Jim Pearce; Jean Rowe; Mary A. Tame; Wendy M. Thompson; Michael Warren; Rex Wild; Abe Woolnough.

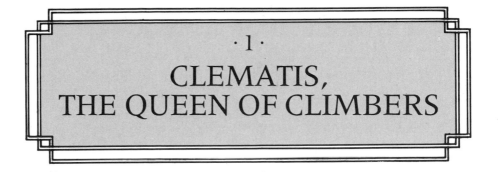

# · 1 ·
# CLEMATIS,
# THE QUEEN OF CLIMBERS

lematis, or the virgin's bower, to give the plant its common name, is surely the most beautiful of all climbing plants and is rightly called 'the queen of climbers'.

Why the popular name is never used these days is a bit of a mystery. In most other plants it is the other way round, the popular name being far better known than the correct Latin one. Indeed, many people are often surprised to learn the correct names of plants they have loved all their lives. Exactly when the plant came to be known as the virgin's bower is uncertain, but most people accept that it was named after Queen Elizabeth I, who was known as the 'Virgin Queen'. Plants of *C. viticella*, the variety found growing wild in Spain, were brought over to England during her reign, and, it is said, named in honour of the queen. Another idea is that it is named in honour of the Virgin Mary as the wild variety found in Britain, *C. vitalba*, comes into flower in August at the time of the Feast of the Assumption, or Lady Day during harvest, which is 15 August. There is an old couplet which says:

> When Mary left us here below
> The Virgin's Bower began to blow.

So you take your pick, but I am sure that it will always be called by its proper name clematis, which comes from the Greek and means 'a vine branch'. Clematis should be pronounced with a short 'a' as in the word 'America', all three syllables being equally accented: *clem a tis*.

To many people the word clematis still means either the small-flowering *montanas* which create such a picture in the spring, festooning everything within reach with their myriad anemone-like flowers, or the purple 'Jackmaniis' covering many a porch with a mantle of royal purple throughout the summer. True, these two varieties are still the most popular and are seen more than any others, but there are many more equally beautiful and perfectly hardy varieties, and with less than half a dozen clematis we can have masses of flowers in the garden from March to October and often, in a mild autumn, through to Christmas. There are even winter-flowering varieties, *C. calycina* and *C. cirrhosa*, which produce charming bell-shaped flowers from attractive evergreen foliage in mild spells from January to March.

So, with a little planning and a bit of luck, the keen clematis grower can have flower the whole year round. And if flowers are lacking during the winter there are always the attractive seedheads to use in floral arrangements throughout the dull dark days.

Clematis grow throughout the temperate regions of the world. The beautiful blue *C. alpina* has even been seen flowering in the north of Norway, within the Arctic Circle. This gives some idea of the hardiness of clematis. In these northern districts they are often cut down to the ground every winter, but the roots remain alive and in the spring will send up strong shoots, soon to be covered with flower during their short summer. In the British Isles they are perfectly hardy and even the severe winter of 1962–63 failed to kill them. Many were cut down to ground level, but they soon recovered in the spring and we had a riot of bloom the following summer.

Clematis belong to the family Ranunculaceae which includes such plants as buttercups, anemones, paeonies, aconites, kingcups, hellebores, etc. Upon inspection it will be found that clematis have no petals, the flower consisting of the sepals which open out with green backs, quickly changing in colour to give us the attractive flower with a central boss of coloured stamens. They climb by means of their leaves, twisting them round their hosts, or round wire and trellis on walls, so space must always be allowed behind these supports to give the leaves a chance to get through and grip. They do not cling to walls, and when grown through trees and shrubs their grip is firm but light, so that they do no damage to their hosts.

The flowers vary in size from the tiny star-like *C. flammula*, which scents the garden during the autumn, to the enormous 10-in (25 cm) blooms of such varieties as 'W. E. Gladstone' and 'William Kennett'. They are also diverse in shape, most of the hybrids being star-like and flat, while in the species there is great variation. Some have bell-shaped flowers, single and double, such as *C. alpina* and *C. macropetala*. Some have tubular-shaped flowers, such as *C. afoliata* and *C. rehderiana*. Some have urn-shaped flowers, such as *C. texensis*. Some, the *montana* varieties for instance, are shaped like an anemone, and some, like *C. recta* and *C. flammula*, are very small and star-shaped.

The species come from many different countries, but the majority are from China, where many plants that we treasure in our gardens are found growing wild. There are over 250 species, but a large number of them are not worth garden space, and only the best are found in nurserymen's catalogues.

The large-flowering hybrids that create such a sensation when seen in full flower are of recent introduction. Before 1850 there were only the small-flowered species, but with the arrival of two large-flowering species collected in China, named *C. patens* and *C. lanuginosa*,

*C. alpina* scrambling over the rocks in the Alps.

*C. alpina*, seen here growing in its native habitat, the southern Alps. (*right*)

*C. alpina sibirica*. The wild white *C. alpina* taken on the island of Mali (Little) Ushkanii in the middle of Lake Baikal in Eastern Siberia, a remote spot seldom visited by Westerners. (*far right*)

*C. alpina* 'Francis Rivis', an improved variety also known as 'Blue Giant'.

the floodgates were opened, and during the latter half of the nine-teenth century hundreds of different varieties were raised, many of them still with us today, such as 'Belle of Woking', 'Henryi', 'Jack-manii', 'William Kennett', etc.

Colours in clematis are varied and beautiful. There are no garish or bright colours, the majority being softer in shade than other garden plants, but they run through a complete range of colours, red, pink, purple, lavender, mauve, white and even yellow. The length of flowering time is much longer than with other flowers; each individual bloom will be at its best for three weeks or more, and when we get the summer-flowering varieties, producing buds from June to September, the effect is of a plant that is in flower for three months or longer. The early-flowering varieties produce all their flowers at once and so do not have such a long flowering period, but they often produce flowers for a second time on the young wood in late summer and autumn, so they also can be said to flower for two months and more.

Many will climb to great heights; the *montanas*, for instance, will cover a 60-ft (18 m) tree in a few years, producing a fantastic sight in May and June. Others will grow only to 6 ft (2 m), such as 'Madame Edouard André' or 'Hagley Hybrid', making them ideal plants for a bungalow or small garden. There are even herbaceous clematis, *C. davidiana* and *C. recta*, which make a small bush of 3 or 4 ft (90–120 cm) and do not look like clematis at all, but are an ideal subject for the border, and sweetly scented too.

Lack of scent is the one failing in the large-flowering hybrids; only one has any real scent and that is 'Fair Rosamund' which has a delicate primrose perfume. The species and the small-flowering clematis do, however, have several varieties with a good scent. Early in the spring the evergreen *C. armandii* is covered with masses of waxy white flowers with a delicious almond scent. Then in May and June the pink and white *montanas* have several varieties which fill the air with almond perfume. During the summer the large-flowering varieties take over and there is a lack of scent, but in the late summer and autumn the species have their turn again. *C. rehderiana*, with its pale yellow tubular flowers, reminds us of the spring with a cowslip scent, and the two herbaceous varieties, *C. recta* and *C. davidiana*, flower well into the autumn. Finally, the best of them all is *C. flammula*, which, with its thousands of tiny white flowers, will scent the whole garden on a warm moist evening. There is a pink variety called *C. flammula rubra marginata*.

The sweet autumn clematis of America (*C. maximowicziana*, ori-ginally *C. paniculata*) also has a scent, as its popular name suggests, but in Britain it is so late in flowering that this is not very evident. As an article in an American newspaper said in 1974:

Without splitting hairs over it you could well maintain that this wild autumn clematis is the most wonderful of all plants. There

*C. armandii* 'Apple Blossom'. This handsome evergreen variety flowers in March and April with masses of delightfully scented pale pink flowers. It is a little on the tender side and needs a warm south-facing wall.

*C. armandii* 'Snowdrift'. The pure white version of this strong climber which will grow up to 20 ft (6 m) and more.

11

is precious little in the natural world that is too good to be true, and gardeners are always conceiving extravagant enthusiasms for some plant or other, only to discover that their marvellous discovery has a few faults they didn't know about at first. This clematis, now blooming all over Washington, is one of those exceptional plants that boasts such a roster of virtues as might make a saint blush and yet it has no faults at all to speak of. One becomes a gardener, we all agree, just about the time it dawns on us that the *C. paniculata* is a far superior plant to its more flashy relatives.

There are two reasons this clematis does not always bring forth the clamour of praise to which its beauty automatically entitles it. First it is common, and that is nearly always a fatal flaw to acceptance by snobs. Second, the English do not grow it well, it cannot abide the dismal climate of these sub-polar islands, and with them it is often ruined by freezes, since their feeble sun does not suffice to bring it into flower until too late.

The English, however, are far less snobbish about their plants than Americans are. If they discover a plant that grows well, has showy or charming flowers and is presentable throughout the year, even when not in bloom, they cherish it mightily. Indeed their diligence in ransacking the world for first-rate plants is unparalleled and it is no wonder the English bear the prize.

Most of which is quite true, but in the south of England, with some of our beautiful autumns, the sweet autumn clematis of America does tolerably well and flowers almost as freely as in Washington, in spite of our 'feeble sun'.

Finally, the season finishes with two yellow lantern-shaped varieties: *C. tangutica* and *C. orientalis*, with their masses of feathery seedheads, both of which do extremely well in the British Isles.

Such then are the diverse forms, habits and beauty of the undisputed queen of climbers and in the following pages I shall endeavour to give some hints on growing, training and looking after these most rewarding plants.

During the summer of 1973 I spent a holiday at Gravetye Manor, near East Grinstead in Sussex. Gravetye! Now here is a name to excite all clematis lovers, for it was here that the famous William Robinson and his gardener Ernest Markham created a wonderful collection of clematis in the 1920–30 period. The garden itself was started in 1885 and completed in 1908, and William Robinson kept a journal about his work during that time. I was allowed to borrow this huge work and was fascinated to read of the planning and the planting of thousands of trees and shrubs. Clematis do not appear very much during the formation of the garden and the only mention of them is in 1893 when he says, 'planted montanas, viticellas, flammulas and graveolens in the hedgerow and rose fence near the garden'. The only plants that remain now are the *montanas*, with

*C. afoliata*, the rush-stemmed clematis, a native of New Zealand. The flowers are daphne-scented and there are few, if any, leaves.

enormous thick stems, climbing through trees and flowering in profusion every spring and early summer.

Large-flowering varieties did not seem to catch William Robinson's fancy until a much later date, when, with his faithful Ernest Markham, he planted many varieties between the two world wars, experimenting with them in various parts of the garden. They also did a good deal of hybridising and produced many new varieties, 'Ernest Markham', 'Miriam Markham', 'Huldine', *C. texensis* 'Gravetye Beauty' and, *C. tangutica* 'Gravetye', to name but a few. These have now all disappeared as the garden was neglected during the Second World War when the manor was taken over by the army. However, strenuous efforts have been made since then by the present owners to restore the garden to its former beauty. They now run the house as a hotel and country club.

I suggested to Mr Herbert, the owner, that clematis should be planted in the garden again and he agreed and suggested that I look round and find suitable spots. The obvious place should have been the pergola, a massive affair built of stone and oak timbers, but William Robinson had built this to take the great weight of wisteria

13

and when I saw it the pergola was enveloped in great writhing stems, suggesting, as one walked through, a weird and gloomy tunnel of fossilised ropes. William Robinson's idea was to have the wisterias eventually climbing through the nearby trees, and here, in 1973, his dream was realised as the trees were all festooned in masses of wisteria flower – an incredible sight. Since then the pergola and its ancient wisteria have both been removed as the pergola was in danger of collapsing.

As the pergola was thus engaged I had to look round for other situations and found an ideal spot at the lower side of the terraced garden. This was a large retaining stone wall with nothing much on it but ivy and one or two plants that would make ideal hosts for clematis. On the south side, which is about 6 ft (2 m) high, we have planted *patens* and *lanuginosa* varieties that need no pruning and which will give a good show of flowers in the spring and early summer. On the north side, which is part of the terraced garden, the wall projects 2 ft (60 cm) above the soil. On this we have planted 'Jackmanii' and *viticella* varieties to scramble along the top of the wall, tumble down the south face and flower from July to October. They can all be cut back hard every winter and make a fresh start in the spring. So there will once again be a wall of clematis at Gravetye, to remind the devotees of the days of William Robinson and Ernest Markham. Many other varieties have been planted in various places in the gardens, on trees and shrubs, so that they will grow naturally, which is the ideal way to grow clematis.

I have in my possession a copy of a slim volume written in 1912 by William Robinson on the subject of clematis and in his introduction he says: 'I have had so much pleasure from the cultivation of these lovely plants that I venture to print a little book on the subject, as one sees even large gardens desolate so far as they are concerned.' I am afraid the same is true today; on visiting gardens open to the public we often search in vain for clematis or are surprised to find even one clematis, often an ancient neglected specimen tucked away in an odd corner. As well as a rose garden, these gardens could easily contain a clematis garden such as is described in Chapter 8, which would add interest for the public and flower from Easter until October.

William Robinson goes on to say:

> I open one Nursery catalogue in which Clematis are divided into thirteen groups, each with an awkward Latin name and some of these divisions are of doubtful value. Needless hair splitting is one of the evils of the pretended science of the day, and in the case of our gardens certainly serves no good purpose. Therefore I treat the family in alphabetical order as the simplest way, and one there can be no garden objection to.

Recently botanists have changed the names of some varieties. For instance, what used to be *C. paniculata* is now *C. maximowicziana*. The name *paniculata* has now been given to the tender white evergreen

'Alice Fisk'. A cross between 'Lasurstern' and 'Mrs Cholmondeley'

New Zealand variety *C. indivisa lobata*. What *indivisa* has turned into I haven't managed to find out yet. Sepals are now called tepals, although I shall still call them sepals. William Robinson has a few words to say about this. He says:

> In botany these technical terms may be essential, but gardening is quite a different matter and for ages the effect of botanical classifications on the garden has not been a happy one. Nor are they necessary. The names in our own tongue are as good as any and we are not prevented from adding the Latin name when necessary. A garden is of all things in the world a place to select. In botany all plants are of equal value, but in gardens we must choose or suffer. If we go in for all kinds, good or bad, we end in a museum or a botanical garden, but that rarely gives us beauty. Therefore I omit all graceless kinds, and those that do not climb.

He then goes on to list all the varieties grown at Gravetye, describing the species in detail and just giving a list of the hybrids, which is rather odd, but I think he preferred the small-flowering species to the enormous hybrids, although he does say about them 'the beauty of these plants is worth any amount of taking trouble to secure' and 'no orchids or other flowers seen at the most famous flower show can equal them for beauty of colour!' I wonder what the orchid growers would say about that nowadays!

This book is written mainly for the thousands of ordinary gardeners who love growing clematis just for the sheer pleasure of seeing their 'traffic-stopping' displays, although most clematis seem to be planted at the back of houses and can rarely be seen from the road. So this book is written very simply, avoiding as many technical terms as possible and following William Robinson's advice. The list of varieties at the end is in alphabetical order, and there is one chapter for the large-flowering hybrids and one for the small-flowering species, just mentioning the confusing groups into which clematis have been listed in the past. This is the only division I think necessary.

So to those who say they cannot grow clematis, or that they are difficult to grow, I would say I hope that after reading my book you will try again, for they are so rewarding. And to those lucky people whose gardens are filled with fabulous clematis, nothing need be said, except to express a little jealous admiration. They have the right soil and the time and patience to water and feed. These are the three essentials for success in growing clematis: the right soil (and this can always be achieved by replacing poor soil, or enriching it with manure, peat and bonemeal); feeding, without which no plant will grow properly or give of its best; watering, one of the most essential 'musts' for clematis as they belong to the buttercup family which grows in moist places and needs gallons of water a week during the summer.

So if you want to grow clematis really well, plant them deep in a good soil with 3 or 4 in (7.5–10 cm) of stem below the soil. Then, during the growing season, soak them with water once or twice a week, and give a good feed of a liquid fertiliser once a week during the growing season, but not when in flower. If you can do this, I guarantee that you will be richly rewarded with plants that will be a source of pleasure and joy to you the livelong spring, summer and autumn.

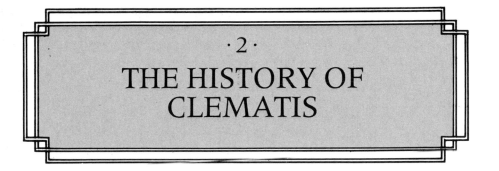

# THE HISTORY OF CLEMATIS

he only clematis native to Britain is *C. vitalba*, or, to give it its many local names, traveller's joy, old man's beard, hedal feathers, snow in harvest, etc. These names refer mainly to the rope-like branches covered with masses of fluffy seedheads which festoon trees and hedges in the autumn. The stems also seem to have been used by boys for smoking in the past, which has earned *C. vitalba* the extra names of boys' bacca, smoking cane and shepherds' delight, although what the taste of boys' bacca was or how they smoked it I have no idea, nor have I ever met any shepherd who has smoked shepherds' dlight, a lovely name but no doubt a revolting habit. On chalky soils *C. vitalba* covers hedges and quite large trees, in fact literally swamping them and presenting quite a spectacle in the fall of the year. These seedheads are in great demand at harvest festival and many a window, font or lectern are graced with long trails of clematis, very few people knowing that it is the native clematis of Britain. This variety has been used in the past as a root stock for grafting clematis (see chapter 6).

This was the only clematis known in Britain until the reign of Queen Elizabeth I. With the spread of trade around the world travellers interested in gardening began to bring plants back from other countries and amongst them were several of the species that are still with us today. *C. viticella* came from Spain in 1569. It has given us many beautiful varieties and has also been used as a rootstock for grafting plants of the large-flowering hybrids. In 1573 *C. integrifolia* arrived from Hungary, a herbaceous variety with nodding blue flowers. The evergreen clematis *C. cirrhosa*, a winter-flowering variety, followed in 1590 from the Mediterranean and from there also came *C. flammula*, the scented virgin's bower, with thousands of tiny flowers. Then, in 1597, the herbaceous variety *C. recta*, or *erecta* as it was originally called, came from south-east Europe. This makes a 3–4 ft (90–120 cm) high erect bush, hence the name, topped by masses of sweetly scented white flowers. It was quite an interesting introduction.

Thereafter nothing much happened for a hundred years until the eighteenth century when travel became a lot easier and botanists began searching the world for new plants to bring back to Britain. A marsh clematis from the USA arrived in 1726, called *C. crispa*, a pale blue, bell-shaped, rather fragile variety, and also *C. viorna*, a herbaceous variety which was urn-shaped and dusky-red, called the leather flower on account of its leather-like sepals. *C. orientalis*, the orange bell-shaped clematis, arrived in 1727 from Asia. In the latter half of that century introductions began to speed up and we had *C. virginiana*, with small white flowers, from the USA, obviously from Virginia and similar to our old man's beard, *C. vitalba*.

China was a great source of new plants and sent us *C. florida* in 1776, a double greenish-white which has been the parent of several double clematis since then and gave its name to the group of double clematis. From the Balearic Islands in the Mediterranean, in 1783, came the interesting winter-flowering clematis *C. calycina*, which brightens up the short days of winter with its pale yellow bell-shaped dainty blooms, and is also a useful evergreen variety, something of a rarity in the clematis world. The alpine virgin's bower, *C. alpina*, arrived in 1792; a real charmer this one with its bell-shaped flowers of a beautiful true blue which the large-flowering varieties have yet to achieve. In 1797 a similar variety arrived from America, called *C. verticillaris*, with nodding purple-blue flowers. It was also known as the belle rue of America, but it is very difficult to obtain nowadays.

The nineteenth century was the most exciting time for clematis lovers as plant collectors brought back many varieties from around the world. *C. meyeniana* from Hong Kong arrived in 1820. Similar to *C. armandii*, this variety has white flowers and is rather tender in Britain. Much more interesting was the large-flowered *C. lanuginosa* which caused quite a stir when it was brought back by Robert Fortune in the middle of the nineteenth century. This has pale blue flowers 8 in across (20 cm), with a mass of white anthers. To add to the excitement, Philip Franz von Siebold arrived with *C. patens*, a large purple variety, in 1850. These two must have caused a major sensation because before this all clematis were small-flowered. Nurserymen pounced on these two large-flowering varieties and began crossing them. From these two varieties have come all the large-flowered hybrids of the present time.

In 1820 *C. campaniflora*, a charming pale blue variety, arrived from Portugal, and in 1831 *C. grata*, a large-leaved variety bearing small bluish-white flowers in the autumn, came from the Himalayas. The herbaceous variety *C. heracleifolia*, with blue hyacinth-like flowers, was found in China in 1837. From New Zealand, in 1840, came the white *C. indivisa*, now called *C. paniculata*, with beautiful white star flowers.

In that same year *C. aethusifolia*, a small slender climber with yellowish-white bell-shaped flowers, came from Mongolia. In 1860 we got *C. paniculata* from Japan, a variety similar to *C. flammula* with small white strongly scented flowers. This I have always known as the sweet autumn clematis of America, so how it got from Japan to

'Barbara Dibley'. A striking variety for any position and ideal for a small garden.

America is anyone's guess, or maybe it is a native of America as well. In any case it is now called *C. maximowicziana* (why I know not), and the name *paniculata* has been given to the New Zealand variety hitherto called *indivisa* – very confusing! In 1860 another variety arrived from Japan, called *C. stans*, a dwarf half-shrubby plant with small nodding white flowers. *C. fusca* was also introduced at that time. This is a herbaceous plant with dark red urn-shaped flowers.

In 1880 *C. songarica*, a non-climbing herbaceous variety with white flowers, arrived from Siberia, and, in 1889, *C. douglasii*, a similar non-climbing herbaceous variety, with urn-shaped lavender-coloured flowers, followed. The last of the species to be introduced in the nineteenth century was *C. tangutica*, the Russian virgin's bower, one of the best of the lantern-shaped late flowering yellow clematis, with masses of silky seedheads.

19

Hybridising had already been going on for some time before these new species arrived and one crossing of *C. integrifolia* and *C. viticella*, produced at Henderson's Nursery in St John's Wood, London, and naturally called 'Hendersonii', is still with us, but goes under the name of *C. eriostemon*, a very attractive variety with nodding lantern-shaped deep blue flowers. The first crossing of the large-flowering varieties, *C. lanuginosa* and *C.* 'Hendersonii', took place at Jackman's Nursery at Woking and produced 'Jackmanii', the well-known purple variety which is still as popular today as it was in 1862 when it first appeared.

What an impression it must have caused in those days! There seems to have been a bit of rivalry at that time as another firm in France, called Simon Louis of Metz, claimed to have produced the same variety the year before and called it 'Splendida'; however, the name did not stick and Jackman's won the day. In fact the French firm even printed a denial of their claim in their horticultural press.

Other nurseries were also engaged in hybridising. Messrs Cripps of Tunbridge Wells produced the lavender blue 'Lady C. Nevill'. Another fine variety still in our gardens was the beautiful white 'Henryi', raised by Anderson-Henry of Edinburgh, and Charles Noble of Sunningdale gave us 'Miss Bateman', a variety still loved by flower arrangers for its green bars on white sepals.

On the continent of Europe *C. lanuginosa* and *C. patens* were producing many new varieties but very few of them have survived. In Britain hundreds of varieties were raised and put on the market with such exotic names as 'Beauty of the Bower', 'Gloire de St Julien', 'Lady Stratford de Redcliffe', 'Souvenir de Cardinal Wise-man', all of which have disappeared, which is just as well with names like that!

A book written in 1877 by Thomas Moore and George Jackman, published by Jackman's Nursery and called *The Clematis as a Garden Flower*, listed 343 varieties! An advertisement at the back of the book says that,

> Since raising and introducing the well known clematis Jackmanii, we have made the cultivation of this flower a speciality in our business, and thus we have been the means of distributing several hundreds of thousands of clematis, through nearly every civilised country in the world. In order to keep up anything like an adequate supply, we have found it necessary to propagate annually from 20,000 to 25,000 plants, and to have a sufficient and extensive assortment of saleable plants for purchasers to select from, we have at least 50,000 plants grown in pots in the open ground, a mode of Nursery culture which secures their safe removal at any period of the year, since they can be transplanted (out of pots) at any season with little or no risk.

The forerunner of the garden centre of today? We think our garden centres, with their containerised plants, are quite modern, but Jack-

*C. calycina*, also known as *C. cirrhosa balearica*, the winter-flowering evergreen clematis.

man's were years ahead of them.

From China in 1900 came *C. quinquefoliolata*, so called because it has five-lobed leaves. The flowers are milky-white and appear in August and September. However, the major new variety of that year was undoubtedly the evergreen *C. armandii*, Armand's clematis, introduced by E. H. Wilson. This lovely climber has large dark glossy green three-lobed leaves which are a feature of this variety. The white, scented flowers appear in April and May. It was named in honour of Père Armand David, a plant collector of the nineteenth century. In 1904 two more varieties arrived from China, a late-autumn-flowering variety with creamy-white flowers, called *C. chinensis* (about time a clematis was named after the country of its origin), and *C. rehderiana* syn. *C. nutans*, called the nodding virgin's bower, a vigorous grower with small nodding pale yellow bell-shaped cowslip-scented flowers, flowering in late summer and autumn.

In 1906 came *C. ranunculoides*, again from China, a herbaceous variety with pinky-purple panicles of flowers in July and August. *C. pavoliniana*, another Chinese introduction, came along in 1908. It is similar to *C. armandii* but not so vigorous, with small white, scented flowers in June. From New Zealand in the same year came the curious *C. afoliata*, the rush-stemmed clematis, so called because its stems are very like reeds. The tubular-shaped pale yellow flowers appear in May and are fragrant, similar to those of the daphne. Another very fine clematis from China appeared in 1909. This was *C. spooneri* (syn. *C. chrysocoma* var. *sericea*), similar to the *montanas* but with larger flowers, pure white with yellow anthers, which appear in their thousands in May and June.

In 1910 *C. chrysocoma* appeared (not to be confused with the previous variety); this one is called the hairy clematis on account of its young shoots covered with golden-brown hairs. It has pink saucer-shaped flowers in May and June and on the young wood in the summer. Also in 1909 one of the most beautiful of the species to come from China arrived in Britain. This was *C. macropetala*, introduced by Reginald Farrer, although it had been discovered in the previous century by another French missionary Pierre Nicholas le Cheron D'Incarville, but not brought to the UK. The semi-double blue nodding flowers appear in profusion in April and May. In 1911 *C. fargesii* made its appearance, again from China, with flowers very similar to that of the blackberry (*Rubus* spp), being small and white and appearing from June to September. Finally, in 1918, came *C. serratifolia* from Korea, with small yellow flowers with red anthers followed by silky seedheads.

Most species, therefore, were discovered by the end of the nineteenth century. Very few have been introduced since the First World War of 1914–18, although some interesting and hitherto unknown species have recently been discovered in China by Raymond Evison, the founder of the International Clematis Society.

Until the end of the nineteenth century and during the early years of the twentieth, clematis continued to be grown in large numbers but then their popularity began to wane as more and more plants started to wilt from the effects of a mysterious disease which has since been called clematis wilt (see chapter 11 for more on this maddening malady). Gardeners began to despair and clematis went out of fashion for several years. Between the two world wars they reached their lowest ebb, in spite of the efforts of William Robinson and his gardener Ernest Markham. Several new hybrids were produced by Ernest Markham in the 1930s and he even named one after himself, or maybe William Robinson insisted that he did so. Ernest Markham also wrote a book on clematis, the first one to appear since Jackman and Moore's book of 1877, except for a slim volume written in 1912 by his employer. Even this seems to have had little effect and it was not until after the Second World War that clematis became fashionable again, mainly owing to the plants being shown at the Chelsea Flower Show by several firms, and new books being written about clematis, the only work available at that time being Ernest Markham's book.

Magazine articles on the subject began to appear, more nurseries began to specialise in clematis and they became readily available in garden centres. New fungicides were produced, such as Benlate, which helped to control clematis wilt. Clematis began to appear on television in *Gardeners' World* and on other programmes which, with the advent of colour television, encouraged the viewing gardening public to try the more exotic-looking varieties and, once bitten, to make collections of these lovely climbers. People also found out that clematis could be grown in many ways beyond climbing the usual garden wall and gardeners began to experiment with growing them on beds of heather, as specimen plants in tubs, and through trees and

'Comtesse de
Bouchaud' flowers
non-stop from June
to September.

shrubs, perhaps the most natural way to grow them.

So we are now seeing a great revival of these graceful and charming climbers and, as more books are written about them, the more the gardening public will appreciate them. Long may they continue, as Michael Haworth-Booth wrote in his book *Effective Flowering Shrubs*, 'to enslave their devotees in a happy bondage which, at least, ensures that never again will they know the curse of boredom for an instant'.

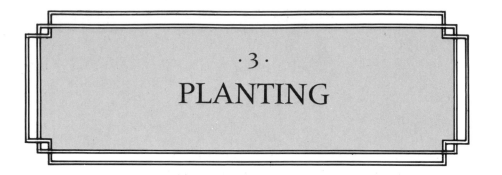

· 3 ·

# PLANTING

ecause very few general nurserymen seem to know anything about them, clematis should always be bought from a reputable firm. A large number are brought in from Holland every year and simply sold as a sideline. There is nothing against this practice, of course; many garden centres do not grow any of the plants they sell, buying them all in. Many nurseries grow plants for sale to garden centres and, as clematis are difficult to raise and take a lot of looking after, this explains why there are so few nurseries that specialise in clematis. However, these nurseries do exist, and you will find them always willing to give you plenty of advice and help in buying your plant. Most of them will send plants to any place in Britain. They pay special attention to packing, as clematis are awkward plants to pack. A planting leaflet will invariably be sent, giving you complete details of how and when to plant.

Having got your clematis, the first thing to do is to choose the site. The flowering period of the variety will give you a clue as to the best aspect, as some varieties will grow in complete shade and some need full sun. Those that flower in the spring and early summer will grow in complete shade, and so are ideal for north-facing walls, but can, of course, be planted on any wall. Some of the summer-flowering varieties will also grow in such a position, but it is best to plant them on an east, west or south wall, whilst those that flower in the autumn need all the sun they can get and a south-facing wall is the best choice for these late-flowering varieties.

Soil does not matter very much as clematis will grow practically anywhere, provided that it is not waterlogged or of pure sand or clay. The ideal soil is a well-drained, rich, friable loam. Very few gardens consist of this perfect combination, but all soils can be improved by the addition of humus in the form of manure or compost. Sandy soils, which are very hot and dry and lose moisture very quickly, can be improved by adding large amounts of farmyard manure, peat or leaf mould, the main idea being to increase the moisture-retaining properties of the soil. Clay soils, on the other hand, already have too much moisture-retaining property and, to improve them, they

24

should be double-dug and the subsoil broken up, adding a fair amount of coarse sand. Dry hop manure and peat mixed well in will also help to make the soil more friable. If waterlogging occurs during the winter it would be advisable to drain the land to take the excess moisture away. Clematis are moisture-loving plants but do not like to have the crown of their roots perpetually in water, especially in the winter. If drainage is impossible, try growing clematis in large tubs or containers with no bottoms. The crown of the plant will be safe in the tub, in some good John Innes compost, while the long tap-like roots will go down to the wet conditions below and not take any harm. Chalky soils are ideal for the species, but hybrids do not do quite so well in them and plenty of farmyard manure and peat should be mixed in when planting clematis.

Having chosen the site and improved the soil, we now come to the important matter of planting. The thing to remember is that you are planting for the future and that your clematis is going to remain in this spot for many years, so it is advisable to spend a little time in preparing its home. When planting young plants, prune them back to the lowest pair of leaf buds, which will be about 6 in (15 cm). If the plants insist on growing one stem only, pinch this back to the lowest pair of leaf buds on this new growth and when they break out with two shoots, wait until they have grown about 10 or 12 in (25–30 cm), and pinch these back again to the lowest pair of buds. This will make the plant nice and bushy, but the nearer the ground the better as, with an annual mulch, the bottom of the stems will root into the mulch and add vigour to the plant.

Clematis are supplied in pots or containers if bought directly from a nursery. If they are sent by post, they will invariably be in a paper pot. Plants are transferred to these to save carriage costs, and to keep the solid pots, which are quite expensive items, to be used again at the nursery. Before the plant arrives you can prepare the actual spot. If this is near a wall, do not plant too close as a wall is a notoriously dry spot and will suck up moisture at an alarming rate, leaving the poor clematis suffering from drought, the main cause of most clematis failure. Plant 2 or 3 ft (60–90 cm) away if possible. The plant can be trained to the wall by means of canes or wires, or the stem can even be laid under the ground to produce roots of its own, all adding to the plant's health and vigour.

Dig a hole at least 18 in (45 cm) deep by 18 in square. Fork over the bottom and add two or three handfuls of bonemeal. Cover the bottom with 3 or 4 in (5–10 cm) of manure, hop manure or compost. If your own soil is good this can be used to fill up again, but if it is poor, discard it and treat your clematis to some John Innes compost No. 3.

Right then, you are now ready for the big operation, but before planting it is a good idea to give the plant a long drink by standing it in a bucket of water for half an hour, or, if very dry, in water overnight. The centre of the ball of soil is often dry and it is surprising

25

how long the water will show bubbles of oxygen. On top of the manure or compost place two or three spadefuls of John Innes compost, or your own good garden soil with some bonemeal added.

If your plant is in a pot it will be necessary to remove this by turning the pot upside down, spreading the fingers of one hand over the soil to catch the plant, and gently tapping the rim of the pot on the spade handle until the plant slips out. If your plant is in a paper pot, then all that will be necessary is to tear the pot away from the roots. The bootlace-like roots will often be found to have twined round the bottom of the pot. Gently disentangle them and place the ball of soil in the hole, spreading out the fleshy roots so that the crown of the plant is 2 or 3 in (5–7.5 cm) below soil level. Clematis root out readily from stems underground, and if a node, or pair of leaf buds, are on the stem below the soil, then you have an insurance against any damage occurring to the stem above the soil. If this is accidentally severed, or the plant wilts, there is always that pair of dormant buds below soil, which will spring into life and soon shoot up to renew the life of the clematis.

People with difficult clay soils should not follow the above directions to dig a hole filled with compost, as this will only encourage water to drain in and fill it. Clematis do not like their roots permanently in water, and the long fleshy roots would soon rot off. Mix clay and compost together when planting and fork a wide area, mixing in sand and peat. If possible, incorporate some good drainage well below the plant, such as stones, broken pots or brick rubble.

Finally, fill in with your prepared soil, treading it down well with your feet. Leave the cane in and lean it towards the wall or shrub it is to grace in the future (Fig. 1). If you have planted in the summer or autumn, leave the plant as it is until the following early spring when it should be cut down almost to the ground in February, by cutting down to just above the lowest pair of buds on the stem. This is done if it is one of the large-flowering hybrids or one of the late-flowering species such as *flammula*, *tangutica*, *texensis* or the *viticella* varieties. These should be cut down to encourage the plant to bush out rather than run up on one stem.

In the chapter on pruning you will find that only 'Jackmanii' varieties need this hard pruning every year and that *patens* and *lanuginosa* should generally be left unpruned, but for this first year all hybrids, whatever group they belong to, should be cut down. If they come up again with one stem, they can always be cut down a few weeks later. Clematis can stand being cut down frequently and will soon shoot up again, adding to the number of shoots and the vigour of the plant.

Clematis that are planted in the spring have often been pruned at the nursery during the winter. If not, cut them down when planting. Even if they have been pruned and are shooting upon one stem only, it will not hurt to cut them down again, always cutting just above the lowest pair of buds on the stem. The only varieties that do not need

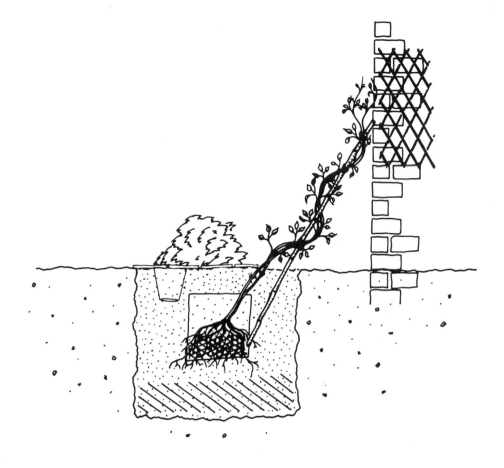

*Fig. 1* Dig a hole away from the wall, 18 in (45 cm) by 18 in (45 cm) deep. Soak the clematis if it is at all dry. Fork over the bottom adding one or two handfuls of bonemeal. Cover bottom with 6 in (15 cm) of rotted manure or compost. Cover with good soil or John Innes Compost No. 3 halfway up hole. Knock plant out of pot, loosen roots if they are wound round bottom of pot. Place ball of plant well down so that two inches of stem are below the surface of soil, which will shoot up from the buried nodes should anything happen to the stem above soil level. Lean plant and fix to trellis or wire support. Fill in with rest of soil and firm down. Use empty pot to sink into soil for watering plant; a tile placed on pot will prevent leaves and debris blowing in. Place tiles or stones on top of soil to keep roots cool and moist.

this initial first spring pruning are the early-flowering species such as the *alpina, armandii macropetala* and *montana* varieties, although this pruning does no harm, as they will send out shoots from the stem, creating a bushy plant naturally. If there is a tendency for the clematis to go up on one stem, prune hard to make it bush out from the base.

### Trees

If you are planting for the clematis to climb through a tree, you need to plant far enough away from the trunk to miss the stongest roots and to avoid the main branches so that the clematis roots will get rained on. The plant can be led into the branches by means of a pole or wire and once in the tree the clematis will weave its way through the branches to emerge all over them (Fig. 2).

We now have the clematis planted safely, but one thing we must do is to make sure the roots will have a cool, moist root run. Clematis do like to have their roots under stones, tiles, concrete or anything that will give them shade and keep their roots cool and moist. The wild clematis, *C. vitalba*, will be found to have its roots in the deepest part of the hedge, protected by the many other hedge plants, where it is usually well shaded and damp. Clematis, therefore, will grow quite happily with other plants, such as roses, shrubs, etc., gratefully accepting any shade these neighbours can provide for their roots.

If they are to grow on their own on a hot sunny wall, then you must give them something to provide shade for the roots. This can be done by placing tiles, bricks, stones, crazy paving or pebbles scattered thickly round the plant to cover a 2 ft sq (60 cm) area. Pebbles or granite chippings are ideal as rain can soak through these and keep the ground moist. One way in which a plant in this position can be helped, if it is in a very dry spot, near a wall for instance, is to sink a pot, level with the soil, beside the plant. Through this the plant can be watered during the spring and summer. Water will not be wasted this way and will go down directly to the roots of the plant rather than running off on the earth's surface.

Clematis do need a tremendous amount of water; their long, thick, fleshy roots will suck up water at an amazing rate and, probably, during very hot spells, they take at least a gallon a day. Water, of course, will wash away the nutrients in the soil and these must be replaced by a liquid feed given at least once a week. This can be given through the sunken pot as well. If this sunken pot looks incongruous in the garden it can be hidden under a small tile which will also prevent the pot filling with leaves and other garden rubbish.

Clematis have very thin stems and are vulnerable in the garden. The misplaced hoe or the over-enthusiastic weeder have often cut short the life of a young clematis. Cats, dogs and children can also be a threat, so, until the plant has established itself, a little protection should be given, such as a neat cylinder of wire netting staked round the plant, letting down an inch or two into the soil. Wind is one of the worst enemies of clematis and, until the plant is established, some form of windbreak is essential. Even a few twigs will stop the full blast of a strong wind, for instance.

A good start in life has now been given to our plant and we must not forget it in the future. Clematis must have a constant supply of water during hot dry spells. Not just a dribble, which only wets the surface, but a real good soaking to get the water down to the roots 2 ft (60 cm) below!

If your soil is good, then an annual mulching of manure each autumn will be sufficient, but, during the summer, feeding with a

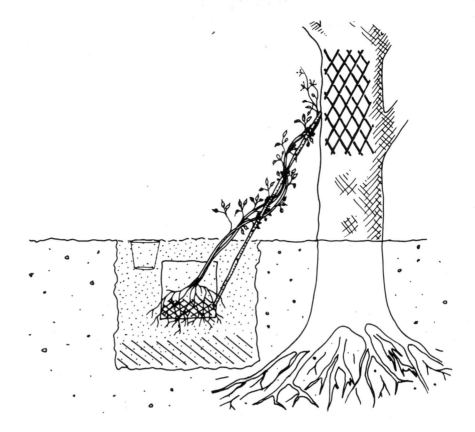

*Fig. 2* If possible always plant clematis on the north side of a tree or shrub, as they like their roots to be in the shade. Plant well away from the trunk to avoid the roots of the tree or shrub. Pot sunk into soil to assist with watering.

liquid fertiliser once a week will replace those nutrients which get washed away with constant watering. Most bottled feeds, such as Sangral, Maxicrop, Liquinure, Phostrogen, etc., are quite all right, and the instructions for dilution are given on each bottle.

Poor soils will require a little more attention. Two or three handfuls of bonemeal should be scattered round each plant in the autumn and worked into the soil with a hoe or hand fork. A mulching of manure can be given as well if possible. Then, in the spring, a handful of sulphate of potash will keep your plant healthy and the foliage a good colour. It also promotes strong growth and can be given two or three times during the spring and early summer. Sprinkle the powder, 2 oz (57 g) to the sq yd (0.8 sq m), round the plant and water in.

So, to put it in a nutshell, plant deep, water often, feed well, and your clematis should thrive and be a thing of beauty for years to come.

# ·4·
# TRAINING

lematis climb by twining their leaf stalks round anything within their reach, even their own stems. Constant supervision will prevent this happening, of course, but clematis grow so quickly that it is often impossible to keep pace with them. However, if you provide the necessary supports for the plants to cling to, then you should be able, by checking at least once a week, to guide them where they should go. In the spring, when growth is rapid, a plant can get into a horrible tangle if left unattended for a few days. On warm growing days a clematis will grow 3 or 4 in (7.5–10 cm), and if these conditions continue for several days the plant will have grown almost 2 ft (60 cm) in a week! So at this time of the year, especially with the 'Jackmanii' varieties, make sure that all the shoots are tied in and trained so that each stem is shown off to advantage and all the flowers can display their beauty and not be lost in the bird's nest of tangled growth that one so often sees. Although clematis will grip tightly to anything their leaf stalks can find, their grip is not a stranglehold. (One will, however, sometimes find a flower on the clematis that has been unable to open because a leaf stalk has wrapped itself round the bud before it had a chance to flower.)

They must, therefore, have something for their leaf stalks to cling to. They do not cling to a wall as ivy does and so they do no damage to walls. The cheapest method for walls is to wire the wall. Plastic-covered wire is better than bare wire that can get hot on a sunny wall and burn the leaves. This can be attached to nails spread about 9 in (23 cm) apart along the top, bottom and sides of the wall, so that the wall is covered in 9-in (23 cm) squares. Nails can be spaced at intervals in the centre to give rigidity and support for the plant. Make sure, however, that the wire is at least $\frac{1}{2}$ in (1.25 cm) away from the wall, so that the leaves have a chance to get behind the wire and twist themselves round it. This is an ideal cheap method when large areas of wall have to be covered. For just an odd spot on a wall there are several makes of wooden, wire, plastic and iron trellis frames that can be fitted to the wall and these are obtainable at most garden shops and centres.

30

The natural way to train a clematis is through a bush or tree. One look at the native British clematis will confirm this, festooning as it does many of our hedges and trees with its feathery autumn seed-heads, especially on chalky soils, which has suggested in the past that clematis are lime-loving plants. Clematis are often said to require hot heads and cold feet and this can be seen to perfection with the wild clematis; all the flowers and seedheads are at the top of the hedge and if we follow the stems down to the roots we will find that they go down to the dampest and coolest part of the hedge at the bottom. This gives a clue when planting on a tree or shrub; plant on the north side, so that the tree will give shade to the roots. Plant as far away from the tree as possible, and lead the clematis into the tree by means of a pole or wire. Alternatively, one could plant the roots well away from the trunk and lay the stem just under the ground so that it will come up the trunk of the tree. To plant next to the trunk itself, however, would be fatal, as the roots of the clematis would have no chance against the roots of the tree.

Many a tree or bush could play host to a clematis and thus play a dual role in the garden. Most shrubs flower in the spring and if you plant one with a 'Jackmanii' variety which is pruned hard in the winter you will have the shrub in flower during May and June while the clematis is finding its way up through the branches. As soon as the shrub or tree has finished flowering the clematis will take over and for the rest of the summer the host plant will be displaying a second crop of flowers – a beautiful and natural way to use clematis in the garden.

A third and very unusual way to grow clematis is on the ground as a bedding plant! The idea is to peg down the shoots so that you get a carpet of flowers all looking upwards, quite an unusual sight. 'Jackmanii' or viticella varieties are the best for this method, as they flower for a very long period and can be pruned hard every winter to give you a chance to clean the bed and work in some fresh manure or fertiliser. Several plants should be used on a fairly large or long bed so that you can train the shoots over blind spots, such as the lower parts of the clematis itself. Instead of pegging the shoots down, wire netting could be stretched over the bed, or pea-sticks laid on the ground, to give the plants something to scramble over. One-year-old plants will take a year or two to establish themselves in such a position and so it is worth while finding two- or three-year-old plants, or using bulbs and bedding plants to cover the soil while the clematis is growing.

An even better method is to plant the bed with winter-flowering heathers. Once they become established they make an ideal plant for clematis to wander over. 'Jackmanii' or viticella varieties should be used as these will flower during the summer and autumn when the heathers are dull. They can be pruned hard in the early winter to give the heathers a chance to flower until the spring, when the clematis will start to grow again and flower all the summer.

Looking down on clematis has inspired one of our Norfolk customers to grow them up higher, on a flat piece of Netlon stretched horizontally across some stakes 3 or 4 ft (90–120 cm) high. The clematis can be trained up these stakes, or on canes, to scramble around on the flat Netlon. Several clematis grow very tall so that all one often sees is the undersides of the flower. As this lady says, 'Only God sees them and why should He have all the pleasure, so I grow them flat, well off the ground so I can look down on them too!'

The pergola (a walk covered with arches) is another method of training clematis and one can easily be erected with a few poles, making an attractive addition to the garden. A more permanent and handsome pergola can be made with brick pillars and this can be wired as described for walls earlier. Poles will also need something attached to them for the plant to climb on, such as wire netting wrapped round them. Three or four single wires stretched between nails at the top and bottom of each pole is a simple and effective method of helping the plants to climb.

Clematis can be trained on tripods of poles at the back of the herbaceous border, or on frames, as a feature in the centre of a bed, but whatever method is used for training, do make sure that the leaves have suitable wires, irons or trellis work of small enough size for the leaf stalk to twist round and that there is space behind these supports for the leaves to curl around two or three times, to enable them to get a good firm grip to support the weight of the plant. Clematis will sometimes grow to prodigious heights, and if pruning has been neglected the bottom part of the plant will be bare. These bare legs take up literally no room, and can be covered by growing a smaller plant – such as a shorter clematis, shrubs or annuals – in a tub placed at the base to give a second level of flowers.

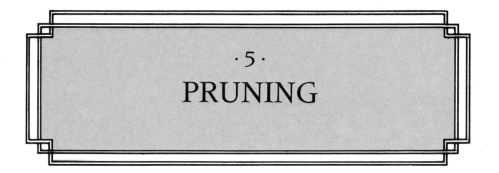

# ·5·
# PRUNING

lematis that flower in the early part of the year do so on the previous year's ripened wood and therefore need no pruning. Clematis that flower in the latter half of the year do so on young wood that has been produced the same season and therefore these clematis need hard pruning every year.

That, in a couple of sentences, is the answer to the question of the pruning of clematis, which, to many people, is still a bit of a mystery. However, it is not quite as simple as that, as some of the early flowering varieties flower again later on in the summer on young wood which they have made since they flowered in the early part of the year, which makes it all rather confusing. The thing to do if you do not know the name of your clematis, is to find out when the main flowering time is, and the way to do this is to leave the plant unpruned for a year. If it blooms freely from April to June it is a variety that does not need pruning and belongs to the *patens* and *lanuginosa* groups. These groups will often flower, during the summer and autumn, on the young wood, but this does not matter; they can be left alone, unpruned but trained, if there is plenty of room, to give each vine space in which to produce its blooms without overcrowding. When they do get out of hand they can be pruned back hard after their main flowering period, which is May and June.

If, however, your clematis starts to grow in the spring and keeps on and on and does not produce any flowers until July or August, and then keeps on flowering continuously until the end of September or October, then it belongs to the 'Jackmanii' or *viticella* groups and needs hard pruning every year. This can be done any time during the winter but must be done before the end of February as clematis start to grow very early in the year. In January, if the weather is mild, shoots begin to swell and by the beginning of April they are well on their way up their supports.

## Spring-flowering plants

Let us return to those that flower in the spring and early summer on the previous year's wood. In this group are a large number of small-

33

flowering species and they have only one flowering period, with no second blooming as the hybrids have. If all early-flowering clematis bloomed only in the spring and early summer then we would know where we were and what to do, but, alas, the large-flowering hybrids that bloom in May and June will confuse the issue by producing a second flowering period on the young wood during the summer and autumn.

The species which only bloom once in the spring include such varieties as *C. calycina, C. alpina, C. macropetala, C. montana, C. spooneri* and their varieties. They all produce thousands of small flowers on the previous year's wood and they need plenty of room for expansion, except perhaps the *alpina* varieties which are not very rampant growers. If you have plenty of space they can be allowed to ramble at will, creating a very pleasing picture in the spring. However, if you have only a small garden and wish to grow these charming early-flowering species, then a certain amount of pruning is necessary to keep these plants within bounds. This can be achieved by pruning directly after the plant has flowered. The plant can be pruned quite hard and, as the growing period of the early-flowering varieties is after they have flowered, the plant has all the rest of the summer in which to produce its flowering wood for the next spring. In this way even such rampant varieties as the *montanas* can be grown in a fairly small space, and even if the plant looks like swamping its allotted space, it can be stopped by cutting back the growing tips when it has filled its area.

When pruning like this it is a good thing to encourage the plant by giving a good soaking of a liquid fertiliser before pruning and afterwards; this gets the young shoots moving. Species do not need as much feeding as the large-flowering hybrids, especially the early-flowering ones, so if the area is limited and the plant is a strong healthy one, these two feedings will probably be sufficient. However, do keep an eye on the growth during the summer, watering well, and if it looks as though a little help is necessary, give it another soaking of a liquid fertiliser.

## The patens group

The *patens* group will be the next to flower. These are the varieties that produce those huge exotic blooms in May and June, such varieties as 'Lasurstern', 'Nelly Moser' and 'The President'. They send out side shoots from the previous year's growth and it is on these that the enormous plate-like blooms appear. No pruning is necessary once the first-year pruning has produced a bushy plant, but careful training is essential, otherwise the shoots will simply rush straight up the wall or support and develop into a horrible tangle at the top. Training clematis shoots can be a tricky operation as the young shoots are very tender and very brittle; too much bending and off they snap. Do not worry too much if this happens, however, as the plant will

'Beauty of Worcester'. The flowers are double in the early summer and single in autumn.

soon send out another shoot, or maybe even two, which will be an added bonus.

On a well-established plant you can do a little light pruning in March or April, cutting back any dead shoots, but here a word of warning is needed; a shoot may look dead and only after the secateurs have snipped through it do we realise to our horror that there were green buds further up the stem. So start from the tips of the shoots and work your way back just to make sure that you do not inadvertently cut off any flowering buds. A lot of dead ends can be removed at this time of the year, but it is not absolutely essential as the flowers and new growth will soon cover up any dead patches. One lady I know prunes her 'Lasurstern' once every three years. She does not touch it for two years, but the third year she cuts it down hard as one would a 'Jackmanii' variety, and at the same time as the 'Jackmanii' varieties are pruned. She gets several smaller flowers on this young wood in late summer, but loses the early flowers for that year. Her plant is thick and bushy, grows up to 6 ft (2 m) and is a mass of flowers in May and June during the two years when it is not pruned. So there are no hard and fast rules for pruning; one suits oneself.

## Double varieties

Double varieties, such as 'Duchess of Edinburgh', 'Belle of Woking', 'Countess of Lovelace' and 'Vyvyan Pennell', will be flowering at the same time. These belong to the *florida* group and also need no pruning. Doubles are not everyone's choice but they are quite popular, especially since 'Vyvyan Pennell' appeared on the scene. Double flowers only appear on the old wood. Later on the plant will produce single flowers on the young wood during the summer – flowers that do not resemble the spring-flowering efforts in the least, often causing people to think that their plants are wrongly labelled!

*C. campaniflora*, the delightful harebell clematis, a native of Portugal.

## The lanuginosa group

The next group to flower is the *lanuginosa* group, which causes more confusion than any other, mainly because many of them flower just as freely on the young wood as on the old (just how infuriating can clematis get!). So with this group you can do as you please about pruning; if you leave them alone, training as well as you are able, then you will get the best of both worlds, spring and summer displays. Pruning, however, will destroy the large blooms that are so effective in the late spring. You can, of course, cut down the plant once in a while, when it is impossible to train any more or the birds have made too many nests, and you will still get a good show in the summer.

If you have a very good plant, furnished with several stems coming from the base, you can try a bit of 'relay pruning'. With this method you cut down half the plant one year, which then shoots up with young growth to provide a summer display, leaving the other half to produce the big early blooms. The following year you reverse the process by cutting down the other side and leaving the part you pruned the year before, thus keeping the plant perpetually in good shape, and obtaining the best of both worlds. You may run into a little trouble with training during the summer, but if you can keep the new shoots of the pruned side away from the non-pruned side all will be well. Such varieties as 'Henryi', 'Marie Boisellot', 'Mrs Cholmondeley' and 'William Kennett' are to be found in this very large section.

## The 'Jackmanii' and viticella groups

The 'Jackmanii' and *viticella* groups can be treated as one for the purpose of pruning. They all flower continuously on the young wood and all need hard pruning every year. That means cutting down to the lowest pair of buds on each stem, often to within a few inches of the ground, especially with young plants. Inevitably this point will get higher from the ground every year, as more shoots are produced, but it does make for a very bushy plant, with many more flowers every year. Therefore, during the winter, preferably in January if the weather is open, proceed with a pair of secateurs to your summer-flowering varieties, bend down and cut through all the stems as low as possible (Fig. 3). Do not look up! If you do you will see lovely fat

*Fig. 3* Summer flowering clematis need this hard pruning every year as they flower on the young wood only. If left unpruned, they will continue growing from where they flowered the year before. Prune hard every winter and before the end of February, weather permitting, as clematis start to grow very early in the year.

buds swelling beautifully at the top of the plant and you will be tempted to leave them. Should you do this you will find that later on in the summer all your plants have bare stems at the bottom without a single leaf as far up as those big fat buds you left the winter before. If left unpruned, your 'Jackmanii' varieties will start to grow from where they left off the year before. This means that if your plant grew up to 8 ft (2.5 m) the previous year, it will start growing from that point, leaving all that 8 ft (2.5 m) below as bald as a coot! They can be left, especially if grown in trees where a bare stem at the bottom does not matter, but when you want to clothe a wall, do please prune hard.

Relay pruning can be used quite effectively in this section to vary the times of flowering. Cut down half the plant at the proper time for pruning in January or February. Leave the other half of the plant until the end of March or, if the spring is cold, the end of April, then cut the second half down. This will result in a much longer flowering period as the first pruning will flower from June to September, and the second pruning will flower from July to October. Varieties in the 'Jackmanii' and *viticella* class include such famous and well-known varieties as 'Comtesse de Bouchaud', 'Jackmanii', 'Perle d'Azur', 'Ernest Markham' and 'Gipsy Queen'.

The late-flowering species need little or no pruning unless space is limited, in which case they can be cut back hard as with the 'Jackmanii' varieties. The herbaceous varieties should, however, be pruned hard every year as, in any case, the previous year's wood often dies back to the ground, so one should cut down the dead stems when clearing up in the garden during the winter. *Viticella* varieties also do best if pruned hard, as, like the 'Jackmaniis', they will start to grow from where they left off the previous year. But the *flammula*, *tangutica*, *rehderiana* or *paniculata* varieties can be allowed to ramble at will, provided you have the room.

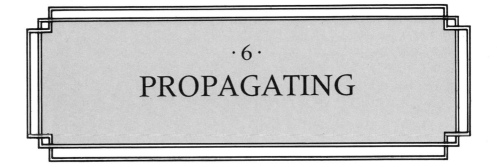

# ·6·
# PROPAGATING

ropagating clematis is always difficult for the amateur. Nurserymen find it easy as their cuttings are taken from young plants which are only one year old. This young thin wood is ideal for striking. Internodal cuttings are used – that is, those without a node or heel at the bottom of the cutting. These soon produce roots in the ideal set-up of the nursery. The amateur, however, has only the cutting wood from established outside plants, which is much thicker than the one-year-old cuttings that nurserymen have, and internodal cuttings cannot be used. So one has to make sure there is a node at the bottom of the cutting as well as one at the top. These take much longer to strike so one must have patience.

To proceed, one needs a sharp knife or a razor blade, rooting hormone powder, a pot, preferably a clay pot, a clear plastic bag or sheet, a watering can, a dibber, and a small bowl of water. The best compost to fill the pot with is a mixture of vermiculite or perlite, or both, some sharp sand and some peat. Mix this thoroughly, watering it to make it moist. Put about 1 in (2.5 cm) of Levington compost or peat at the bottom of the pot, into which the roots can descend and feed the cuttings. Fill up the pot with the moist compost, firm it down and you are ready to insert the cuttings.

The best time of the year to take cuttings is May and June. Cut a stem from the plant you are hoping to strike and, with your sharp knife, cut off the tip of the shoot, which will be too soft to strike, down to where it is firm and semi-hard. At the bottom of the stem the shoot will be too hard and is usually brown in colour. This should also be trimmed off, leaving the centre portion which may produce three or four cuttings according to the length of the stem. With your knife or razor blade cut close above the first node and underneath the node below, making a cutting of 1–2 in (2.5–5 cm) long. Cut off the bottom pair of leaves close to the stem and one leaf at the top, leaving one leaf to keep the cutting going until it is rooted. If the leaf is too big it can be cut in half. Dip the bottom inch (2.5 cm) of the cutting into the water and then into the rooting powder, shaking off any excess powder. Insert the dibber at the side of the compost and put the

*Fig. 4* Clematis cuttings are internodal; that is, without a heel or joint. They are taken from the middle of a stem as the bottom is too hard and the tips too soft. If leaves are too big, half can be cut away. Fill pot with cutting compost and push cuttings in round edge of pot. Cover pot with polythene bag, leave for two weeks, remove and take off any dead leaves and water if dry. Replace or renew polythene bag, repeat procedure, and after a few weeks the polythene bag can be left off and the cuttings potted on into small pots.

cutting in this hole with the leaf pointing inwards, making sure that the bottom node of the cutting rests on the bottom of the hole.

Get the cutting as low as possible, but not so low that the bottom node is in the peat. Then, with the dibber, firm the cutting in the compost. Continue round the pot with as many cuttings as can be fitted in, but not so that they are overcrowded (Fig. 4). Water the cuttings in thoroughly with a fungicide such as Benlate, leave them to drain and dry and then slip the polythene bag over them, tucking it in below the pot. If you have a soil warming bench in the greenhouse, this is a great help and will encourage rooting. If not, stand the pots in a warm but shady spot in the house.

Remove the polythene bag after two weeks, turn it inside out, take off any diseased leaves and spray with a fungicide. Leave until they have dried. Cover the pot again, first making sure that the compost is moist, if not give it a watering, but the polythene bag should keep the compost moist for some time. Remove the polythene bag every two weeks and, after a month or so, test to see if the cuttings have rooted by gently tugging a cutting. If it stays firm then roots have been formed and you can leave the polythene bag off for longer periods until, after a few days, you can take it off altogether.

Keep the cuttings moist by spraying them every day if it is hot and sunny; in dull weather this will not be necessary. Once the cuttings are weaned off, which will be in about two or three weeks, they can be potted into small pots in some good compost. Keep them close for

'Crimson King', a good red clematis flowering in New Zealand.

the first few days in a frame, or cover them with polythene, spraying them occasionally to keep the leaves turgid. Give them some air for an hour or two each day until they look fit enough for you to leave off the covers. This all depends on the time of year. In the autumn the cuttings could be potted on into large pots, keeping them in a greenhouse or some shelter for the winter, and planting them out in the spring. If it is late in the summer when they are potted into the small pots, then it is best to leave them as they are until the spring, keeping them in a frame. They are perfectly hardy and will stand several degrees of frost, but if you are worried about them, simply cover them up with peat for the winter, potting them up into larger pots in the spring and keeping them in a cool greenhouse or shelter for a few weeks before planting them out into the garden.

## Seed

Seed is another way of propagating clematis, but as only a few of the species will come true from seed it is a very unpredictable business. Hybrids will not come true from seed at all and one gets all sorts of peculiar and uninteresting varieties by this method, but it is in this way that good new varieties do sometimes occur, as described in the chapter on hybridising.

One of the snags of seed sowing is that seed takes anything up to three years to germinate, except for some of the species which will come up the same season. *C. tangutica* and *C. davidiana*, for instance, germinate very quickly.

Seed should be gathered in the autumn, on a dry day, as soon as it is ripe, put into a paper bag (not plastic) and kept in a cool dry place. In the spring it can be sown in a seed-sowing compost in seedpans or pots. Larger seeds can be sown fairly deeply, but small varieties, such as *tangutica* or *davidiana* need only just covering.

Most clematis seeds have long tails on them which make up the attractive seedheads; the seeds are joined together in a tight ball with all the feathery tails sticking outwards. This ball of seed, when dry, can be broken up for sowing in the early spring. Seed with only small tails can be sown fairly easily but some of the hybrids are more difficult to cover and it is perhaps a good idea to dibble them in with their tails sticking up out of the ground. At least one would not sow too thickly by this method. Once the seed has germinated and the first pair of leaves appear, lift them carefully out of their pan and pot each individual seedling into a John Innes No. 1 or Levington potting compost. If nothing has appeared by the early summer, stand the pans outside on the north side of a building, so that the sun does not bake them bone dry, and leave them there until the following spring, letting them weather with frosts and snow during the winter. This will sometimes encourage them to germinate quickly when brought into the warm greenhouse in the following spring.

## Grafting

Grafting is a commercial method now used less and less by nurserymen. Before the Second World War most nurseries employed the grafting method to propagate, but since it has been discovered that clematis will grow equally well from cuttings, grafting has fallen out of favour and most nurseries now rely on internodal cuttings to produce their plants. The one advantage of grafting is that a plant grafted in March will be a saleable plant in July and will flower well the first year. We always graft a certain number of plants, mainly to quickly produce new varieties and to provide a good show of flower from July to September when many visitors are about in the coastal area of Suffolk where we live.

The opponents of grafting have always suggested that this method encourages clematis wilt, but this is nonsense. They say that the grafted plant is not on its own roots, to the great detriment of the clematis, but again this is not true because a clematis is not grafted permanently on to its stock. The stock is simply used as a nurse stock to get the scion over its first six months, after which it will develop its own roots. By the time the clematis is planted in the autumn the scion will have taken over and the root stock will be discarded and will die away during the winter; provided, of course, that when potting on the young grafted plants from small pots into large ones, the union is potted well below the level of the soil in the pot.

Clematis are grafted on to the native English clematis, travellers' joy, or, to give it its correct name, *C. vitalba*. Seed of this is sown outside in drills in the spring, and the seedlings are fit for grafting in their second year, which means that the scion has a two-year-old root to supply it with all its needs for those important six months. These wild clematis are lifted in the winter and brought into a frame

'Corona', flowering in a New Zealand nursery.

or cold greenhouse with their roots covered with peat or soil to encourage them into gentle growth. At the same time plants of the variety to be propagated are brought into a warm greenhouse to encourage them to produce 3 or 4 ft (90–120 cm) of strong young growth. When this has happened, usually in March, they are ready for grafting and a handful of stocks are brought in ready for the operation.

Before beginning, some thin pieces of raffia are soaked in water to make them soft and pliable. The young growth of the named variety is prepared by cutting it into sections, one pair of leaves to each section, which will provide two scions each. The top growth of the stock is removed and a suitable straight part of the root is selected for grafting. A clean straight cut, about 1 in (2.5 cm) long, is made along the side of the top part of this root, just paring off the bark. The section of the hybrid is then prepared by cutting straight down between the pair of buds, leaving the leaves on, and thus giving two scions. The cut is then tapered off to fit the cut on to the stock; a simple way of grafting known as whip grafting. Carefully fit the scion to the stock, making sure that the bark fits on both sides, for it is here that the union takes place. Hold the stock and scion together and bind them firmly but gently with the raffia, taking a turn or two above the bud and then tying round and round until you reach the base of the cut where you finish off with a half hitch.

Trim off any part of the stem and scion sticking up above the binding and your graft is complete and ready for potting into a 2½-in (6 cm) pot in John Innes compost No. 2 (Fig. 5). Place the pots in a shaded propagating frame with bottom heat and keep them close for three or four weeks in a temperature of about 65°F (18°C), looking at them occasionally to see if they need watering, or to make sure that

43

*Fig. 5* Clematis can be grafted on to the wild clematis *C. vitalba* ('Traveller's Joy'). Sow seed of this variety in early spring and in two years time, plants will be fit for grafting. This is done in March in a warm frame in a greenhouse. To provide scion material, bring plant into warm greenhouse in February. After grafting, pot into small pot, leave in frame for about three weeks, when a small bud will appear at base of leaf stem. Harden off gradually and pot into larger pot.

the leaf is not damping off. Spraying with Benlate will prevent this.

After three weeks look at the bud at the bottom of the leaf stalk, which should by now be swelling. When it is ½ in (1.25 cm) high, it is time to take the pots out of their close quarters and to a more airy bench in the greenhouse. Keep them shaded when the sun is shining as the March and April sun can get very strong through glass and will soon shrivel up the tender little shoots. When they are 3 or 4 in (1.5–10 cm) high they should be given little sticks to support them and pinch out the growing tip, to encourage them to break into two shoots. Clematis are very hardy plants and do not like too much heat, so, as soon as possible, put them into a cooler house and ventilate well on hot days.

They are now ready for their final potting into 5-in (12.5 cm) pots. Use a Levington compost or a John Innes No. 3, making sure when potting to see that the union is below the level of the soil in the pot. There is little else to do, except to stake each plant with a bamboo cane, see that it is kept well watered and fed at the proper time, and tie the plant to its stake as it grows. By July it will be at the top of the cane and in bud, and you can either keep it in the greenhouse, or plant it outside in its permanent position. If you are not ready for this yet, it can be plunged in the ground outside in its pots; that means digging a hole or trench covering the pot completely, which will keep it moist for the summer, and then planting it out in the autumn.

## Layering

The best and easiest method of all for increasing clematis is by layering. There is no need for greenhouses, bottom heat, stocks or special soil. All one needs is a well-developed plant with several stems that can be lowered down to the ground and layered at the point of impact with the soil. This can either be done by layering them directly into the soil, adding a little sharp sand to encourage rooting, or by

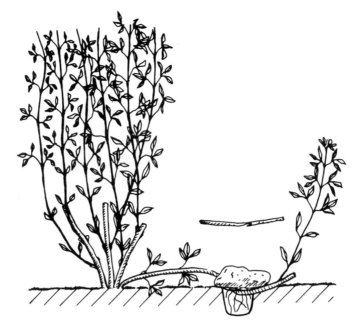

*Fig. 6* The best time to layer clematis is in late summer when the stems have ripened. Where the stem touches the soil, sink a pot filled with good compost mixed with sand. Scrape a sliver of bark off the stem at this point, dust with a hormone powder and peg into pot with a bent piece of wire. Then cover with soil and place a stone or brick on top to prevent layer springing up; more than one stem can be layered at a time. One year later in the autumn, you can cut the stem through on the plant side of the layer and you have a new clematis plant.

sinking pots, containing some John Innes No. 3, into the ground and layering directly into the pots so that when they are lifted, in a year or eighteen months' time, the roots are not disturbed.

August is the best month for layering as the wood has ripened by then. Sink as many pots filled with good soil as there are vines to layer, bend each vine down to the soil, making sure that, when bending, too much strain is not put on the vine, which may snap. At the point in the stem where it touches the soil in the pot, make a lengthwise cut along the bark and dust this with a hormone powder to encourage rooting. A twist can be made instead of a cut, making sure you break the bark only and not the vine. Prepare some pieces of stout wire, bent double to form a hairpin, and peg down the vine in the pot. When this is done, cover the pot with soil and place a stone on top to keep the layer from springing up. The plant must be kept well watered and fed every week, and the pots of soil must not be allowed to dry out. Apart from that, leave the plant alone for a year or eighteen months! What could be simpler?

At the end of this long period of time, try tugging the end of the vine which was left sticking up out of the soil, and if it stays firm the layer is successful. Sever the vine on the plant side of the pot, lift the pot from the soil and, lo and behold! a well-rooted plant to put in another spot or to give to a friend, doing the poor nurseryman out of business! (Fig. 6)

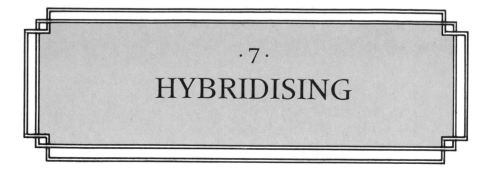

## ·7·
# HYBRIDISING

he large flowered hybrid clematis of today are the direct result of the crossing of the two large flowered species, *C. lanuginosa* and *C. patens*, collected in China in the mid-nineteenth century. Most species come true from seeds, but hybrids do not, and must therefore be perpetuated by cuttings, grafts or layers. Nowadays most large-flowering hybrids are the result of the cross-fertilising of two other large-flowering hybrids, the idea being to get the best out of both plants. For example, when we first raised our variety 'Alice Fisk', we crossed the varieties 'Mrs Cholmondeley' and 'Lasurstern', obtaining the shape of 'Lasurstern' with the colour of 'Mrs Cholmondeley'.

The early-flowering varieties, the *patens* and *lanuginosa* varieties, will produce seedheads readily and sometimes, if sown, these will produce a good new variety, although they will also produce a very large majority of inferior varieties which have to be thrown away.

To produce a new variety using two selected varieties one should wait until the bud of one of them is just about to open, then, with a pair of sharp scissors, carefully remove all the petals (or sepals as they are really called). The anthers which produce the pollen must also be removed and this is done by cutting through the stamens, leaving just the central stigma on the end of the pistil. To prevent any pollen getting on to the stigma, the whole bud, or what is left of it, should be enclosed in a polythene or muslin bag. Within a few days the stigma will be in a viscid receptive state ready for the transfer of pollen from the plant we have selected. To find out if it is ready, remove the polythene bag to inspect the stigma. It should be shiny and covered with a sticky fluid. (This fluid traps the pollen and transmits it down the pistil to the ovary, where fertilisation takes place and seeds are formed.)

When all is ready, choose a sunny day if possible and bring the chosen flower, which should be full out, and gently shake the pollen from its anthers on to the stigma of the other plant. One can also cut the stamens off the chosen plant and shake the anthers over the stigma, or the pollen can be transferred by using a soft camel-hair brush, making sure that the stigma is well covered with pollen.

46

If a cross is required from plants of two different flowering seasons, then the pollen of the first variety of flower, produced, say, in the spring, can be kept in an airtight container in a very dry place until the flower of the second variety comes out later in the summer.

When the operation is complete, cover the stigma again with a polythene bag for a few days to make sure that no stray pollen is transferred. If one is not sure that the operation has been successful, it can always be repeated in two or three days' time. Leave the polythene bag on for a week or two until you are sure that the fertilisation has taken place and there is no risk of a stray pollination. Then it can be removed to enable the sun and air to ripen the seed, which usually takes about four months. It can either be sown immediately and placed outside to winter, bringing the seed pan back in the spring, or it can be stored in a paper bag in a cupboard during the winter, sowing in the spring in either a greenhouse or frame.

Do not expect anything to come up immediately, or even in a few weeks' time. Clematis seed will often remain dormant for a year or two! So if you are an impatient gardener, give up the idea of raising a new clematis. Even when a new seedling appears, it takes another two years before the plant will flower! So it is a very long job, the whole operation taking three or four years before we can see the results of our efforts! Not too long to wait, however, if the results are as good as some of those which have appeared in the last twenty years.

Once the new variety has flowered and you are sure that it is worth growing, it can be kept true by means of cuttings, layers or grafts. You can then give it a name, perhaps even naming the plant after yourself, or a near relative. Nurserymen are always keen to get new varieties and if your plant is good enough they will introduce it to the general public for you, by listing it in their catalogues. You will then have the thrill of seeing your name listed among all the other clematis and, if it is a very good plant, you will have the gratifying pleasure of knowing that your name will go down to posterity.

There are endless possibilities in the hybridising of clematis. Most of the colours in the clematis world are in the pastel shades and if we could simply intensify these colours it would be a great step forward. Do we want a scarlet clematis or a bright yellow one, I wonder? Most people would say no, but a clematis to rival the bougainvillea would really be something. Varieties that are wilt-resistant would be a major breakthrough, and varieties that are bushier in habit would also be a great attraction for the bungalow owner. The future, I am sure, will hold many exciting changes in the clematis world.

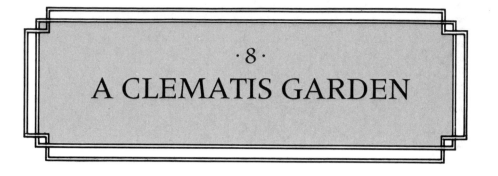

· 8 ·

# A CLEMATIS GARDEN

n suggesting a clematis garden I realise that one of the main uses of clematis is to grow and mingle with other plants; they seem to like the company and many a rose, honeysuckle or shrub acts as a host to a clematis, thus giving a double ration of flowers, with the shrub flowering in May and June and the clematis following on during the summer. The host plants, in their turn, help to hide the bare legs of some varieties of clematis.

The idea of a garden of nothing but one particular type of plant is not new. The rose garden has been popular for many years and there are other types of plants that lend themselves to the creation of a special garden, such as heathers and alpines, but very few people seem to have planted and maintained a clematis garden. This was first suggested in Jackman and Moore's book of 1887 when the name for such a garden was a 'climbery'! No wonder the idea never caught on with a name like that! The idea was again suggested in 1935 in Ernest Markham's book *Clematis*, but seems to have had little success.

## A pergola

The pergola is a feature of many a garden but this usually consists of roses, honeysuckle vines, etc., with the odd clematis planted here and there. Very few pergolas of clematis are ever seen. We have one here at the Westleton Nursery, built with brick pillars and wooden poles and there are clematis in flower on it for most of the year. The only snag of growing clematis on poles or pillars is the wind; with a pergola in a sheltered position all will be well, but in an open spot the wind can often damage young shoots and flowers. In this situation the species are perhaps the best; smaller flowers withstand the buffeting of the wind much better than the huge exotic blooms of the hybrids.

Even with species one can have flower for several months of the year, starting with *alpina* and *macropetala* varieties in April and May, following with the *montanas* in May and June and even into July with the late-flowering *C. montana* 'Wilsonii'. The height of the summer is rather bare of species, except for *C. eriostemon* which flowers all

48

summer, but some of the 'Jackmanii' and *viticella* varieties could fill this blank season with such varieties as 'Etoile Violette', 'Huldine', 'Jackmanii', 'Margot Koster', 'Madame Julia Correvon', 'Margaret Hunt' or 'Venosa Violacea', all good strong growing varieties that stand up to wind and give masses of flowers all summer.

To finish off the season two species will begin flowering in July or August. These are the yellow *C. orientalis* and *C. tangutica*, both producing a fine display of seedheads in the autumn. Later on the *viticella* types, with their delightful saucer-shaped blooms in various shades of purple, pink, mauve, white and crimson, will cover pillars and poles with their dainty flowers well into the autumn. For scent the very small *C. flammula*, with its myriad minute flowers, will give the rich fragrance of almonds, especially on days that are warm and laden with moisture. To take us almost up to winter the late-flowering white *C. maximowicziana* will give us clouds of small white flowers right into November. Thus we can have a pergola in an open position covered in flower for nine months of the year.

A pergola in a more sheltered spot can experiment with many of the large-flowering hybrids and if we can alternate pruning with non-pruning varieties, we can stagger our flowering periods over the whole length of the pergola. The sight of a well-trained non-pruning variety such as 'Nelly Moser', 'The President' or 'William Kennett' flowering from top to bottom of a pole is a sight one will never forget – a veritable pillar of flower. Even in our sheltered position we should find room for at least one of the *montanas*. A splendid new variety, not so rampant as the others in this group, is *C. montana 'Freda'*. This has attractive coppery-coloured foliage and deep cherry-pink flowers, paler in the centre, giving it the appearance of a small 'Ville de Lyon', and is ideal for the pergola.

So much for the pergola, which most gardens can quite easily accommodate, but what about a complete clematis garden?

## A walled garden

If one has a walled or fenced garden, then this is ideal, as one can clothe all the walls with different varieties for flowering at different times of the year, the north-facing wall being reserved for early-flowering varieties which will do well in this position. The space between each plant will vary according to size and vigour, but a general rule is to keep them 5 ft (1.5 m) apart. The walls must be wired or trellised in wood slats, smart modern panels, or wire coated in plastic, as described on page 30.

The central space of a walled garden can be lawn if the garden is small, with perhaps a lily pool in the centre to give a focal point, and with a garden seat at one end where the busy gardener can, once in a while, relax and contemplate the beauty of the clematis family. If the garden is large, then you have the opportunity of growing clematis in a number of different ways. A pergola running both ways, in the shape of a cross, with perhaps a statue or round seat in the centre of the cross, would make a superb setting for clematis of all classes.

In the equally divided four sections you could have clematis raised on tripods made of poles. Here you could grow some of the summer-flowering varieties which can be cut down to the ground during the winter, giving you a chance to treat the poles with a wood preservative such as Cuprinol, but *not* creosote, the fumes of which linger on for months, killing the tender shoots of clematis. Surrounding these you could have beds of the herbaceous varieties, *C. davidiana, C. integrifolia,* or *C. recta.*

## A bed of clematis

An even better and much more exciting idea is to have beds of clematis on the ground, treating them as bedding plants, an effective and unusual way to grow them. This was first used over a hundred years ago when, at Jackman's Nursery at Woking, a batch of 'Jackmanii' plants were blown down in the early summer and the poles were not renewed. During the summer it was noticed that the plants spread out over the ground and flowered profusely. The effect was so dramatic that special beds were prepared where the clematis were pegged down to the ground, and for several years these beds of clematis were a famous feature of the nursery. A hundred years later we have copied this success and in the centre of the lawn at our nursery in Westleton we have a clematis bed of various 'Jackmanii' and *viticella* varieties.

If used as a central feature the bed should be at least 15 ft (4.5 m) in diameter, to give the plants plenty of room to be trained to cover the ground and to allow for the planting of six or more plants in each bed. 'Jackmanii' or *viticella* varieties should be used to give continuous flowering from June to October, but the summer-flowering varieties must make a certain amount of growth before they flower. There are always bare spots, so if one has six or more plants dotted over the bed, they can be trained over each other and tied down to cover the bare spaces. During the summer they will flower for an incredibly long period, giving a massed effect, and at the end of the season, or during the winter, they can be cut back hard (Fig. 7).

The beds can be planted permanently with bulbs which will give a covering of colour in the spring, and, while the bulbs' leaves are dying down, the shoots of the clematis will be covering the beds to blossom all summer.

## A heather bed

An even better way of growing clematis on the ground is to grow them over a bed of winter-flowering heathers. These low-growing plants make an ideal anchor for clematis to scramble over and they do no damage to their hosts. If the summer-flowering varieties are used, such as 'Comtesse de Bouchaud', 'Etoile Violette', 'Hagley Hybrid', 'Madame Julia Correvon', 'Madame Edouard André', 'Margot Koster', 'Prince Charles', 'Ville de Lyon' and the lovely *viticella* varieties, then they can be pruned hard in the winter, giving the heathers a chance to flower until April, by which time the clematis will have started into growth and strong stems will be shooting up all over the bed.

It is best to leave these shoots to fall over on to the heathers naturally. They are so brittle at this stage that if you try to bend them over to train them to where you want them to go, they will snap off nine times out of ten. So leave them to go their own way and once they are lying on the heathers you can encourage them to go in the direction you want them to so that the bed is evenly covered.

Someone will no doubt point out the fact the clematis are lime-loving plants and heathers are lime-haters; true, but fortunately clematis will grow quite happily without lime and, as long as they are watered well during dry spells, they will be quite happy. Another objection will be the fact that clematis like feeding and heathers do not and often will not flower if fed. If your soil is poor, sink a 5-in (12.5 cm) pot close to each clematis, then water directly to the roots of the clematis and give an occasional liquid feed through the pot as

*Fig.* 7 Clematis can be grown on the ground as a permanent bedding plant. Summer flowering varieties are best as they flower non-stop for a long period and can be pruned back hard in the winter. Bulbs can be planted to give early season colour, or winter flowering heathers can be planted over the bed which will give the clematis something to ramble over. This illustration is of clematis on wires stretched over and fixed to small stakes to keep the plants just off the soil.

51

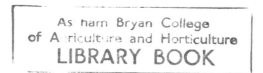

*Fig. 8* Clematis make ideal tub plants. A fairly large tub should be used, if possible, as they make a good root system. They can be kept out of sight until just coming into bloom, when they may be placed on the patio, etc, and be an attractive addition to the garden. Use good soil or John Innes Compost when planting, and make sure they are kept well-watered if it is at all dry. Clematis are moisture-loving plants and must also be fed generously whilst growing, but not, however, when in flower.

well. This will go down directly to the clematis roots and the heathers, being shallow-rooted plants, will not be affected by the water or feeding. If the soil is good, then, with the clematis suggested, it will not be so urgent to feed as these varieties are tougher and do not need so much looking after as the huge early-flowering hybrids.

In the centre of the bed a tripod can be erected to hold a central floral pillar, or a herbaceous variety such as *C. davidiana*. This method would be most suitable for a small walled garden where there is not room for a pergola, and a round bed in the centre of a well-kept lawn would certainly be an unusual feature in a clematis garden.

## Tubs

Clematis can also be grown in tubs which can be dotted about the clematis garden. The tubs must be big enough: 18 in sq by 18 in deep (45 cm × 45 cm) is the ideal size, a smaller tub would be all right but would require constant watering and liquid manure. Good drainage

*Fig. 9* Two clematis can be planted on a wire arch, one each side, of different colours, or mixed with a climbing rose or other climbing plants. Clematis like to grow with other plants who act as a host to the clematis.

is essential and the tubs must be filled with a good compost, such as John Innes No. 3. For training the plant a simple arrangement of a 6 ft (2 m) bamboo placed at each corner and tied at the top can be used, or one can obtain a more permanent and decorative iron frame, but whatever method is tried, the result is very worthwhile and can be moved to any part of the garden at any time to fill in a blank spot, used as a specimen plant to stand on a terrace, or even brought indoors while it is flowering. Take them into the open air as soon as they have finished flowering, however, as the clematis is essentially an outdoor plant and will only tolerate being inside for short periods.

Almost any variety can be used to grow in a tub but I think that the 'Jackmanii' or *viticella* varieties are the best as they can be cut down hard every winter, the frame removed and repainted and the tub stored outside behind the scenes, only to be covered or brought inside in very severe conditions. The flowering period of these varieties is so long that they make the best tub plants and will give you a pillar of flowers for months on end.

## · 9 ·

# FISK'S CLEMATIS NURSERY

his chapter is nothing whatsoever to do with how to grow clematis! So you can skip it if you like. It is as much my autobiography as the story of Fisk's Clematis Nursery; how I started it, and the various events that happened on the way. Christopher Lloyd in his book *Clematis* says,

In 1975 Jim Fisk brought out his second volume on the subject, calling it *The Queen of Climbers*. It contains many splendid colour photographs and much good sense. Also a lot about Jim Fisk and his business! It is always delightful to write about oneself. I never tire of it!

So still not tiring and, in fact, adding to the events that have happened since 1975, I have the temerity to repeat it here. The original book was written for our customers and published by the nursery, so it seemed natural to write a chapter on the nursery and its history. I was all for omitting this chapter from this book but the publishers thought it would be a good idea to keep it in, as a bit of light relief I suppose. Anyway here goes:

I fell in love with clematis when working at Notcutt's Nurseries at Woodbridge, Suffolk, in my teens. Woodbridge is only 20 miles (32 km) from Westleton and I had digs there, cycling home for weekends. In 1936 James Coles & Sons of Thurnby, Leicestershire, wanted a propagator to start off their new greenhouses and I applied for, and got, the job. I stayed there until war broke out, joined the navy and served in coastal forces, mainly in the Mediterranean, for five years. When I was demobbed I had the princely sum of £80 gratuity from the government and decided to stay at home at Westleton and start a nursery of my own. This caused great consternation at Coles but as a compromise it was agreed that I should go back there for a time and get the greenhouses working again, building up a stock of plants of various varieties until another young man, who had worked with me in the greenhouses, was demobbed from the army and could carry on. I then returned to Westleton and, to help me start on my own, Coles sent me down a number of clematis stock plants. I was to grow a certain number of clematis for them every year, and each autumn they came down and took a lorry-load back with them to Leicester.

My brother had a very large garden in the village and I had part of this on which my father helped me build a small greenhouse. He was a carpenter and his family were the local wheelwrights, undertakers, etc. During the evenings we would go down to the carpenter's shop where I had to saw the wood with a handsaw while my father made the sections up. Then we pushed them on a handcart through the village to erect them in my brother's garden which was at the other end of the village at the top of a hill!

We had no transport of any kind in those days and the village had no mains water or electricity. I used to catch all the water I could off the greenhouse in a large galvanised tank. When this ran out I had to push a water-cart, which we had picked up for 5 shillings at a sale, down to the village pond and then pull it up the long hill through the village to the greenhouse. The summers of those years I seem to remember as being long, hot, dry and sunny, and it seemed that every day I was hauling up a water-cart from a gradually shrinking village pond!

I had a part-time job at this time which was very suitable, that of village postman. There was only one delivery in those days, which meant that directly I had finished cycling round the village, about 9 a.m., I was free for the rest of the day and could spend my time in my greenhouse growing clematis. This arrangement worked well for three or four years until the Leicester firm got back on their feet after having grown nothing but food supplies during the war. They had a new propagator by now and found that they could grow all the clematis they needed, so I was completely on my own and had to look round for fresh markets.

Fortunately I had been growing bedding plants as well as clematis in my small greenhouse and frames, and had built up quite a good local trade in the spring for bedding plants. Brooms grew naturally well in my brother's garden, which was on the edge of the heathlands that are such a feature of the Suffolk coast, and in the autumn Notcutts would come with their lorry and take all the brooms I could supply. I still grew clematis, of course, and I put some small advertisements in the classified column of the *Nurseryman and Seedsman* and sold several clematis wholesale to nurseries. Customers coming in for bedding plants became interested and started to buy them and so, I thought, why not start a clematis nursery; why not call it 'Fisk's Clematis Nursery', and so we were born. The nursery really dates from 1950 as at that time I was able to buy a plot of land next to our cottage in Darsham Road, lower down in the village, and employ a local boy, Donald Denmark. The only land we had was a very small garden, not much bigger than the size of the cottage, but in 1949 the farmer whose land adjoined the cottage offered me half an acre of land and so, in 1950, we built a greenhouse and office, moved down from my brother's garden and proudly announced in the local paper,

*The Leiston Observer*, that 'Fisk's Clematis Nursery' was opening for the sale of clematis and bedding plants.

I was running the local Sea Scouts at that time, with my friend Charlie Alexander, who was the postman at Dunwich, the village next to ours on the Suffolk coast. We had started with the scouts after the war, finding civvy street very dull indeed, and just after we had built our new greenhouse and office in Darsham Road, the Festival of Britain came along in 1951. We decided to do our bit with the scout troop and we arranged a carnival week during the summer. Our new office with its garage and some old farm buildings still standing next door was ideal as the headquarters for this carnival and stayed so for several years, as the carnival became an annual and very popular event. I am afraid more energy and enthusiasm were put into making torches for the torchlight parade and decorating the carnival queen's float than into the nursery.

The scouts used to come up to practise pageants and plays and the office was full of costumes, props, etc. We had no secretary in those days and I did all the office work myself in the evenings. All the letters were written, and bills and catalogues all sent out after normal working hours. By 1953 the Sea Scouts had ceased to exist, mainly because I hadn't the time to do both jobs, and so the boys used to come up during the summer and give me a hand potting up, staking and tying, etc., and in the winter evenings they would come into the office and listen to the radio and play records while I was typing. They were an energetic lot and often friendly fights would break out and bodies would be wrestling all over the floor while I calmly carried on doing the office work. My customers of those days would have been amazed at the conditions under which their letters were written. All this came to a sudden stop when I acquired a secretary, Gillian Alexander, the daughter of my fellow-scoutmaster and postman. A proper youth club was formed about this time and so all the unruly tenants of my office were able to dissipate their energies in table tennis and badminton. The nursery began to sober up, we became more respectable and we began to grow up.

We built all our own greenhouses. The first three were built in 1950, 1951 and 1952, and these were glasshouses which are used nowadays as the propagating houses. The walls of the glasshouses are 4-ft (120 cm) brick walls with 9-in (23 cm) piers and we became quite good at brickwork as time went by. Building the corner was always the tricky part and as it was my greenhouse I had to do the corners. When we had built the walls for the first glasshouse my father congratulated me on the fact that we were only an inch out, but we made up for that with a spot of cement when putting on the wooden plate to support the rafters. Glazing was another job we had no experience of, but we soon found out how it should be done. Cutting the glass was the greatest worry to everyone until I tried my hand at it and found I had the knack. So I had the job of glass-cutting as well as building the brick corners for all three greenhouses. The

*C. davidiana* makes a small bush, ideal for a border, is sweetly scented and attracts the butterflies.

houses were heated with coke boilers and so we also had to find out how to fit pipes together. By the time we had finished building the three glasshouses we were jacks-of-all-trades — carpenters, brick-layers, glaziers and plumbers.

The lost city of Dunwich lies 2 miles (3 km) to the east of West-leton. It was once the capital of East Anglia with its own bishop, member of parliament, churches, etc., but it all lies under the sea now except for the ruins of a monastery and a small village. I have spent many happy hours on the beach at Dunwich. Four of us young men would cycle down almost every evening in the summer to swim and then call in at the local pub, the Ship, which had a piano in the back upon which I used to thump out the popular tunes of the day.

One of these friends bought a field in Dunwich at that time, opposite the ruins of the monastery. He hoped to start a smallholding there. We all envied him his good fortune as it had a marvellous view of the village and of the miles of marshland and seashore sweeping round to Southwold, an unchanged gem of a seaside town, the whole view overlooking Sole Bay where, three hundred years ago, a mighty sea battle was fought between the Dutch and the English fleets.

Things did not work out for Bruce as he had anticipated, however, and he had to give up the idea and return to his native Yorkshire. He suggested to me that I might like to buy this field from him and have my nursery at Dunwich. I was thrilled at the idea of owning a piece of land in our beloved Dunwich and without thinking of where the money was coming from I said 'Yes', hoping I should be able to raise the necessary before the date of completion. This I was unable to do but I still signed a cheque hoping for a miracle and then found myself in real trouble with a bouncing cheque! Frantic 'phone calls between my solicitors, the bank and myself eventually sorted things out and I was able to increase my already large overdraft. The field was mine!

I then had the crazy idea that I would like to live on that spot with its marvellous view. No more cycling down to the beach; I should only have to walk a few yards. My father and mother both fell in with my plans, especially my father who had always been in love with Dunwich, and so I arranged for a mortgage from the local District Council who offered me £2,000, which we thought was most generous, until a further letter arrived the next morning saying that there had been a mistake and the figure should have been £1,000! However, in those days that was enough to get by with and we ordered a Colt cedar bungalow. My father, being a carpenter and wheelwright, was able to organise everything and with the help of a local builder we all pitched in and built it ourselves, becoming quite expert as we climbed over the roof nailing on cedar shingles, which gave us the name of the bungalow, 'The Shingles'.

Getting plans passed was a bit of a problem as Dunwich is in an area designated a beauty spot, but we built the house at the far side of the field, 200 or 300 yards (270 m) from the road, and it blended in well with a wood next to the field. This wonderful view was now mine and every time we went down during that winter I used to think how happy we would be there. My father, Donnie, Bryan and I would cycle down every morning and by the spring we had almost finished. We decided to have a house-warming party at Whitsun and we moved in the week before.

However, when we eventually arrived down there to stay and did not have to return to Westleton that night I had a dreadful sinking feeling in my stomach and realised I had made a ghastly mistake. The nursery was still at Westleton as we were not moving this down until the summer and I used to cycle over there in the morning and back at night, and this sinking feeling got worse and worse every time I approached our brand-new cedar bungalow. What it was about the place I shall never know but I could stick it no longer and confided in my mother who, to my amazement, said she felt exactly the same and was hating every minute of it. My father, on the other hand, revelled in the peace and solitude of the place and would spend hours just gazing out to sea. However, hearing of our dislike of the place, he agreed to move back to Westleton, where our cottage had been up for sale with no one showing the slightest interest, which was lucky for us, and which is a marked change from today when property in the

'Dr Ruppel', a fine variety from Argentina.

village is snapped up at ridiculous prices.

So we found we could not live with a view and, much to the amazement and amusement of the Westleton people, we came back after three weeks in Dunwich. I did not know it at the time but on the way back into Westleton my mother was sitting in the back of the lorry, full of our belongings, playing 'Home Sweet Home' on our small organ! So we were back in Westleton where the nursery has helped to put the village on the map. The bungalow was put up for sale, and Donnie and I crept into the sale-room at the back and heard 'this desirable residence with a magnificent view' sold for £2,900; not very much but enough to clear my overdraft for the time being.

In those early days, however, customers were few and far between and although I still had the post round, I had to look elsewhere for some money, so we mortgaged the cottage. I was warned by one or two well-meaning friends that once the banks had 'got hold of me' I was on the slippery slope and they would never let me go! Actually I could not have had better friends and all the managers at my local bank have been most helpful, even when we slipped dangerously down that slippery slope some years later and owed the bank and our creditors several thousand pounds. The bank manager came over that Christmas to see what could be done, and as we went through the books, over a glass of whisky, his face became grimmer and grimmer, and it was only my complete self-assurance that everything would be all right, and my smiling face (partly helped by the whisky), that finally persuaded him to give me another chance. Frantic letters were sent to all our creditors with promises of payment in the summer when 'all would be well', and drastic economies were introduced in the nursery, which even meant that I had to hunt through all my pockets on occasions for the price of a drink at the local! This finally pulled us through, and within three years we had crept back into the black, much to my bank manager's amazement and to my great relief. I used to tell a previous bank manager when things didn't look too well that 'next year would be the year' and this happened so regularly that it became a byword between us. He has retired now, but every time I see him he says, with a twinkle in his eye, 'Is this the year?'

One of the reasons for this slide so deeply into the red was our habit of doing everything ourselves; it worked with most things, but not when we tried to install an oil-heater into our coke boiler in the propagating house. It was not properly adjusted and fumes leaked into the propagating frames; we lost our entire stock of young grafted plants, over 5,000 of them. We had to buy in almost all the clematis we needed for sale that winter! We went back to coke the following year!

Another reason, a year or two later, was because we tried to copy the Dutch method of growing clematis. We had seen it working in Britain and were sure we could make it work on the coast of Suffolk. The method is to put cuttings into double glass frames outside in

'Duchess of Edinburgh'. This double white flowers in May and June with semi-double flowers in the autumn.

June. When they have rooted, remove the frames to harden off the plants and keep them growing during the summer. Then, in the autumn, dig them up, pot them into 5-in (12.5 cm) pots and plunge them outside, that is bury the pots underground in neat rows in beds about 2 ft (60 cm) wide. We could get as far as this, but the growing of the plants outside was never a great success. We put the blame on the close proximity of the sea. Salt air will penetrate up to 15 miles (24 km) inland, especially when there is a persistent east wind, such as we often get on the east coast in the spring, and young clematis do not seem to care overmuch for salt air, although a mature plant will stand it quite well; I have seen several well-grown plants only 100 yd (91 m) from the sea.

After two years of trying these methods, failing and having to buy in several thousand clematis each autumn, I realised something had to be done. Fortunately I have always been an optimist and I was sure that I could get things round. I had a brilliant idea. On the nursery we had a hundred Dutch lights, many with broken glass. I thought up a plan to cover these with polythene and build two large green-houses by standing these Dutch lights on end and bolting them together to form the walls. We put a roof of polythene over them stretched on wire netting supported by the rafters. They were 60 ft (18 m) long and 20 ft (6 m) wide and we had all our clematis under cover. Each house held over 6,000 clematis and they grew beautifully during their first season. The whole operation had cost very little and the houses were built during our quiet time, December to March.

These two large polythene houses have now been taken down and in their place we have several long tunnel houses. These tunnel houses are the cheapest, most efficient and the easiest to erect of all the greenhouses we have seen, I only wish they had been invented many years ago! They are simplicity itself and can be erected in a couple of days by two quite inexperienced men. They are available in kit form and consist of ten or twelve iron hoops which are fixed into the ground, correctly lined up of course. A trench is then dug on each side of the house. A huge sheet of polythene is then stretched over the hoops, preferably on a warm, calm day. The edges of one side of the polythene are placed in one of the trenches which is filled in to hold the polythene down. The polythene is then pulled tight over the iron hoops, the opposite edges are put in the opposite trench which is filled in and hey presto! you have a green-house. To complete, it is necessary to make a door at either end to which the ends of the polythene sheet can be attached, thus making a very neat and efficient job. We have fourteen polythene tunnels and find them ideal for growing clematis, so if you are interested and are near our village, do call in and see them.

These tunnel houses are not heated like the growing houses as clematis do not need any heat once they have been grafted or the cuttings have been rooted and potted up. Our three original glass-houses, which are now the propagating houses, are heated with oil and electricity, a wonderful, efficient and labour-saving method. When they were first built, we had small coke boilers outside each house, and many is the cold winter night that I have had to go down through the snow or rain to stoke up the boilers, only to find in the morning that the temperature had dropped to a dangerous level.

Our first show was the Suffolk Show at Benacre Park in 1955. This was the annual agricultural county show which was held in a

*C. flammula,* or the scented virgins bower scents the whole garden in late summer and autumn.

different part of the county each year. Actually this was almost its last move as it has had a permanent site at Ipswich since then. The Suffolk Show is held on the first Wednesday and Thursday in June and consequently is an ideal place to exhibit clematis as many of the *montana* varieties are still in flower and the large-flowering hybrids are just at their best.

As we were not too well known at that time we had several

clematis left over from the previous year plunged outside in the ground, usually in neat rows with wire stretched round every cane to hold them firm during gales. Plants left over from the previous year and plunged for the winter often develop large flower buds at the top, and these can be used for shows during May and June, some slight forcing for May-flowering varieties being needed. My father built me some wooden tubs and 6-ft (2 m) wooden trellis-work to fit at the back of each tub. We knocked the plants out of their pots and filled as many as we could into these tubs, all the pink 'Nelly Mosers' in one tub, all the white 'Henryi's' in another and so on, taking the canes out and training them up the trellis-work. All we had to do then was to transport them to the show, arrange them on our allotted space to create the best impression, and have a catalogue stand in the front containing our first catalogue with pictures (black and white at that time, of course).

We had no lorry to transport these clematis the 15 miles (24 km) to the show and so had to hire one, as at that time we did not even possess a car; bicycles were our only mode of transport then and remained so for several years. We were extremely lucky with our first show, however, as the Queen Mother happened to be the royal visitor and one of her favourite flowers is the clematis, so, naturally, when Sir Arthur Penn, who escorted her round the flower show, came to my stand, they stopped and admired and bought several plants.

Sir Arthur Penn lived only a few miles from the nursery, and was a customer of mine, so a little more luck entered into the occasion, especially as the Queen Mother was staying with him! I remember Sir Arthur telling me after the show how delighted Her Majesty was with her reception in Suffolk. The may flowers (hawthorn) were in full bloom just then and the hedges were white with blossom, and as she drove to the show the Suffolk people tore off branches of may to wave as she went by.

One exhibitor at the show was rather annoyed with me. He had been going to shows for several years and had never had an order from the royal family nor even spoken to them and on my first show the Queen Mother not only stopped and spoke to me but gave me an order as well! He was livid but has forgiven me since.

Clematis had never been shown in Suffolk before and so, naturally, we got a good amount of publicity. A photograph of our stand appeared in the *East Anglian Daily Times* the next morning, showing me taking an order from a customer and mentioning our royal order. This really started the ball rolling; other local flower show organisers were interested and we were asked to go to Ipswich, Norwich, Colchester and Yarmouth Flower Shows during that summer. As we had no transport we had to look round to see if we could find something suitable and in a local garage we found a very old black van which we bought for £50. We still had no driver but an old school friend, George Church, who lived in the village, offered his services, and

*C. fargesii* var. *souliei* is ideal for growing through evergreen shrubs.

used to drive Donnie and me to these early shows, often helping on the stand when one or other of us had to go off for meals. He knew nothing about clematis but what he lacked in knowledge he made up for in enthusiasm and he encouraged several people to buy clematis. What happened to the nursery while we were away at these early shows I am not quite sure. We used to come home every evening, none of the shows being more than 40 miles (64 km) away, but I have no doubt that my mother and father took good care of it and saw that the watering was done and the ventilation put on in the greenhouses.

Our local shows were so successful that we moved our sights further afield and during the next year or two we exhibited at such places as Shrewsbury, Southport, Leamington Spa, Bristol, Windsor and the Royal Horticultural Society fortnightlies at Vincent Square in London. Our Black Maria was obsolete by now and we had to look round for something more reliable. We found an Eastern Electricity Board lorry which cost us £80 and filled our needs completely. It had a canvas roof supported by iron hoops, which came in very useful as we used to sleep in the back of the lorry. We could not afford hotels in those days; our two hammocks were lashed to the iron framework at either end of the lorry and we would sleep in great comfort and cook our breakfast on a primus stove the next morning. Donnie, the young lad who worked for me, had learned to drive by this time and I was learning, so we carried an L-plate on the lorry all over the country. The furthest afield we ever went was to the Highland Show in Scotland. This show also moved about the country before it had its permanent site at Edinburgh, and the year we decided to go it was held at Dundee. One of the reasons for this long journey was that a friend of mine in the village, Sam Kennedy, came from Glasgow, and he suggested that we could stop at Glasgow and spend the night with his people. We could go on to Dundee the next morning, leaving him to spend a few days with his relatives, and pick him up on the way back. We left Westleton at midnight on Saturday – Sam and Donnie decided to drive through the night while I could sleep in the back of the lorry, which worked very well. I slung my hammock across the lorry at the back where there was a little space and, as they say in the navy, 'I got my head down' and slept throughout the night. I woke up the following morning to find the lorry at a transport café at Scotch Corner where we had our breakfast.

Feeling much refreshed, I said, 'Right, I'll take the wheel now and someone can get his head down and have a rest,' so into the driving seat I got, started up, drove out of the car-park, turned in the direction I thought we were going, and Sam shouted, 'Where are you going?'

'To Glasgow,' I replied. 'No, you're not,' said Sam, 'you're going back to England.'

So we had to turn round and point the other way and drive over the hills of Westmorland in the blazing heat of a perfect June day. Our lorry had one fault, the brakes would sometimes bind and we would have to crawl underneath occasionally to bleed them, and sometimes, as the brake-drums got very hot, we would have to stop until they cooled down. This, of course, happened during our struggle over these hills and we stopped for almost an hour, lying on the bank resting in the sunshine. We aimed to get to Glasgow in time for tea, but within a few miles of the city we found the main road completely blocked for repairs to a bridge and we had to go miles round the Devil's Beef Tub, up more hills and down narrow tracks before we reached Glasgow for a late tea, a hot bath and bed. It was a very warm night, almost Mediterranean, and as I lay in bed thinking of our journey there came one of those magical moments I shall never forget. It was at the time when Pat Boone's records were popular and down the street someone came singing one of Pat Boone's songs, getting louder and louder, completely unaffected. The song, beautifully sung, faded away in the distance as I drifted into sleep.

Donnie and I travelled on the next morning to Dundee where we set up our exhibit, but we did very little business; most people came and looked and admired the clematis but said, 'Och, they'll no do up here!' Of course they do 'do' up there but we could not persuade

*C. florida bicolor (sieboldii).* This fascinating variety needs a sheltered position or can be grown in a conservatory. (*right*)

*C. florida alba plena.* The double white variety. (*far right*)

many people that, in spite of their exotic appearance, they were perfectly hardy. Still, it was a very enjoyable week. One of the highlights of the show was the concert held every evening in the stockmen's canteen, when several of the stockmen went up on the stage and did some turns, and very good ones too.

We continued to tour the country for the next year or two, as by this time I had increased the staff and we had Brian Baggott and Philip Holmes working at the nursery. Now we were able to send two people to a show while the other two remained at home looking after the nursery. We started to exhibit at the RHS fortnightly shows about this time, but here we were unable to sleep in the lorry. We stayed, however, with some very kind friends, Mr and Mrs Arthur who lived in Dulwich. We had been introduced to them through clematis, when, on holiday locally, they had visited the nursery, and hearing we were hoping to exhibit at Chelsea they very kindly offered to put us up. We stayed with them for several shows, parking the lorry in their front drive at night, and joining in the rush hour into London every morning, leaving the lorry on a 'bomb-site' car-park in Westminster all day. We returned in the evening to Dulwich where Mrs Arthur would have prepared a sumptuous meal for us, after which we relaxed in the garden or the drawing room, chatting to our charming hosts and generally unwinding before going to bed where we dropped off to sleep, almost before our heads had touched the pillow.

Before exhibiting at Chelsea we had to prove to the RHS that we could put on a good show, and I remember an autumn show we went to at Olympia when one judge said, 'If he wants to come to Chelsea he'll have to fill up the space better than that.' We used to bring our exhibits to shows already arranged. My father had built us some wooden trellis screens which were nailed to a long narrow box at the bottom of the treillis. In this box we stood all the pots and covered them with peat, the flowers and foliage being trained up the trellis-work. It looked very effective and was easy to transport; two of us could lift it out of the lorry and set it down on our site and hey presto! we had an exhibit. We would often arrive at the show at the last minute, when the officials had almost given up hope. The other exhibitors got to know our prefabricated exhibits and, as closing time drew near, they would tell the harassed official, 'Don't worry, Fisk's will be here at the last minute.'

At the Olympia show we were given a site in the galleries, which we hung with a black back-cloth, and we covered the bench with black cloth as well. On this we stood our four trellises to form a crescent-shape exhibit, with two poles at either end in a round bed covered with the red 'Ernest Markham', with plenty of black space all around. In the centre we had a bowl of clematis blooms and we thought it one of the best shows we had ever done; the trellis only filled half the site, giving an impression of light and space. This, to the judges, was a waste of space, they thought that every inch should be filled with flowers and so for our next show at the RHS Hall we filled every available space with flowers, bringing up branches of old man's beard, cut out of the hedge on the way up to London, to cover any bare spots; we even hung the feathery seedheads over the front of the stand. And so we got to Chelsea the following year! (The TV people at Olympia, however, liked our stand, and when we came back from the pictures, having finished our stand in record time and having nothing to do, we heard that the BBC had been filming and our beautifully spaced exhibit appeared on TV the following evening, which proves that not everyone likes to get floral indigestion.)

In our exhibits at Chelsea we tried to exhibit clematis growing naturally, and we built a 20-ft-long (6 m) pergola of hollow wooden posts with hollow cross-pieces at the top where many pots were hidden, to hang their stems and flowers down over the arches. Pots were hidden beneath a peat bed at the bottom of the posts, the canes removed and the plants tied up to the posts to give an effect of them always having been there. Many visitors would come up and say, 'How on earth did you get this up here?' Between the posts we had short imitation walls made of hardboard, covered with 'brick' wallpaper, with a hardboard parapet of imitation 'stone' wallpaper, and down inside these walls we kept all the catalogues. A pair of imitation stone steps at either end led to a raised path through the pergola, under which were hidden all the canes that had been taken from the plants. The whole exhibit was surrounded by beautiful green turf, which had to be brought specially to Chelsea as what little turf there is in the hospital grounds is worn away every year by thousands of pairs of feet walking round all day for a week.

*C. fosterii.* A very rare New Zealand variety which needs a sheltered spot in the garden, or can be grown in a conservatory.

This pergola became quite a feature of Chelsea and on one occasion it almost stopped the Chelsea Flower Show being staged. Three members of the staff, Donnie, Philip and Teddy, had gone up on the Friday before the show to erect the pergola (all the plants were to follow on the Sunday) and as they were screwing on the cross-sections at the top of the pergola a union official came along and asked to see their union cards! Apparently all the carpentry at Chelsea has to be done by union members and exhibitors are not allowed to use a screwdriver on their stands. Of course they had no union cards but, after a heated argument, a compromise was reached. The pergola was almost up and the union official suggested that if it wasn't finished by the time he came round again he would call everyone out on strike. Needless to say the pergola was finished in record time and after that we made sure that it slotted into position and that no screwdriver or any other tool was needed!

We varied our exhibit sometimes by making a round pergola and once we brought up a thatched lych-gate, which is still in the nursery, covered with *montana* 'Pink Perfection'. We never got a Gold Medal at Chelsea, though, in spite of the fact that photographs of our pergola appeared in newspapers and garden magazines. The judges still liked their exhibitors to fill up their allotted space completely, and as we insisted on having space around our stand, the highest award we ever got was a silver Gilt Flora, the next best thing to a Gold anyway.

The idea of exhibiting at Chelsea was not to get medals, however, but to get orders, and in this we were very lucky. We had four members of the nursery on the stand the first two days at Chelsea and we were hardly ever able to speak to each other, we were so busy talking to people and taking orders and by the end of the day we had writer's cramp and were exhausted. By this time our friends in Dulwich had converted their house into two flats and as we now brought four or five people up to Chelsea we had to stay at hotels. We would take it in turns at 6 p.m. every evening, for half the staff to leave and go off to a show and a meal in the West End, the other half staying on until 8 p.m., getting a meal somewhere and staggering in to the hotel and our beds, dead-beat. We had to get up early the next morning as Chelsea opens at 8.30 a.m. and the stand needed a check-up before business could commence, so here again we took turns, two of us getting an early breakfast and wandering down half-asleep to Chelsea, leaving the others for a lie-in to recuperate. I was half awake one morning when dressing, and just after we had opened up I glanced down and saw I had odd socks on! I turned to Cis who was on with me that morning and said, 'Look', and slowly lifted my trouser legs to display one blue and one brown sock; the customers must have wondered what was so funny that morning and I had to go through the whole day with odd socks!

We gave up exhibiting from 1970 to 1974. Ted and Cis, who were keen on shows and had lived with me and worked at the nursery for four years, had gone back to Hertford to live; Gillian and Frances in the office, who also enjoyed the shows, had married and were leaving as babies were on the way, so our regular and seasoned exhibitors all left at once. Teddy, who had been with me to many shows but hated them, suggested that in the circumstances we should stop showing and advertise instead. My brother Jack and his wife Sheila had come to live with me in the place of Cis and Ted but knew little about clematis. So we decided to give up shows and, with our smaller staff, stay at home and see what a few adverts would do instead. To my great surprise and to Teddy's great delight the orders came in thick and fast and we did as much business as we used to do when we dashed all over the country.

However, by 1974 orders began to slow down and it became obvious that we needed to show our face to the public once again. 1975 was also our silver jubilee year and I was rather anxious to get back to Chelsea again and put on an exhibit to celebrate this event. We also had our two new varieties, 'Gillian Blades' and 'Gladys Picard', named after our two secretaries, to show the world. So Teddy reluctantly agreed to go up to London once again, provided that we put on only a small exhibit – no pergolas, rotundas or thatched lych-gates, just plants in flower in pots standing on a staging, which is a very simple way of exhibiting clematis and one that allows the plants to be sold at the end of the show, thus covering our expenses. Our two secretaries came up for the first day and thoroughly enjoyed taking orders for themselves and hearing people remarking how beautiful 'Gillian Blades' and 'Gladys Picard' were. Even Christopher Lloyd said that they looked nice and pretty at the Chelsea Flower Show – the flowers, not the secretaries, of course, although on second thoughts they both looked nice and pretty! The show was a huge success and Teddy has been only too pleased to withdraw his

*C. orientalis* (for close up see page 113). This variety can be left unpruned if there is plenty of room, or pruned hard if space is limited.

opposition to Chelsea, so we hope to be there every year in the future.

The end of that Chelsea Flower Show on the Friday afternoon has to be seen to be believed. Stands that were selling their plants had been besieged by crowds of people for over an hour, waiting for a bell to ring at 5 p.m. This signals the end of the show and that selling time has arrived. The next hour was bedlam, with people waving £5 and

71

£10 notes at us and the exhibits that had taken hours to put up disappearing rapidly as plants were sold at reduced prices as fast as we could go. In less than an hour most of the plants had gone and we were totally exhausted, but at least we had paid for our hotel bill, taxis, lorry, eats, etc., and we went home actually showing a profit.

Since then we have changed our exhibit once again and now take up four 6-ft-long (2 m) trays with trellis attached, as we did when we first started showing in the 1950s. Plants are put in the trays and trained on to the trellis-work. All this is done at the nursery a few days before the show so that the plants are looking natural by the time we get up to London. We also have posts with a tray at the bottom; these are also decorated with clematis at the nursery. On the Saturday before the show all these are loaded into a lorry and on Sunday morning off they go to Chelsea. On being unloaded they are placed on the stage allocated to us, and, apart from labelling and a little arranging, our exhibit is finished and we can have a look about and see everyone else rushing round madly to get finished in time. With this prearranged exhibit we cannot sell off any plants at the end of the show, but we can take orders during the last hours which we were previously unable to do, having been surrounded by eager buyers for about two hours. We can also bring these trays and posts home and stand them in the nursery outside the offices for about two weeks, so that our customers who have been unable to visit Chelsea are able to see part of our medal-winning exhibit.

The home of the Aldeburgh Music Festival is at Snape Maltings, a few miles inland, where one of the large malthouses has been converted into a beautiful concert hall seating over 800 people. A two-week festival is held here every year in June, and other musical events are staged at various times throughout the year, one of the most popular being the Promenade Festival in August, when all the seats near the stage are removed, 300 or 400 people bring cushions and sit on the floor, and a different concert is held every night to suit all tastes. The rest of us more elderly patrons sit in the seats that rise up to the back of the hall. When the hall was first converted I suggested to Benjamin Britten that clematis would look nice round the Maltings and help to soften the exterior. 'Ben' as everyone knew him locally was delighted with the idea and gratefully accepted my offer.

The Maltings were built in Victorian times and the front is a long black wall with a deep 2-ft (60 cm) drain built along the bottom of it. No clematis could be planted there, so we built twelve large wooden tubs made of elm, 18 in (45 cm) deep and square, an ideal size for clematis. These fitted just nicely into this drain, standing on bricks to allow free passage of water underneath. On the backs of the tubs we nailed twilmesh panels which hold themselves up beautifully. We planted mostly white clematis such as 'Marie Boisellot', 'Henryi', etc., and for the first year they did quite well and we paid a weekly visit to water them.

On the east-facing wall we planted species in between the dressing-

'Hagley Hybrid',
known in America as
'Pink Chiffon'. A
good plant for the
small garden.

room windows overlooking acres of marshland going directly out to sea; a wild and grand view. These included various varieties to flower throughout the season, such as *C. montana* 'Wilsonii', *C. montana* 'Marjorie', *C. tangutica*, *C. orientalis*, *C. texensis* 'Duchess of Albany', *C. viticella* 'Minuet' and *C. viticella purpurea plena elegans*. These have grown and flower extremely well in spite of their bleak and open aspect, and they bring pleasure to the many people who attend the concerts throughout the year and to the hundreds of holiday visitors who visit the area each summer.

Alas, two years after the Maltings were opened a disastrous fire destroyed the concert hall during the June festival and we had to rescue our tubs of clematis and take them back to the nursery. They were returned with new plants when the Maltings had been rebuilt the following year and they have been a feature ever since.

Plants in tubs must be watered regularly of course otherwise they will dry out and die, and one hot summer we forgot to go over for two weeks. Although they faced north and were shaded, they had completely dried out. The soil in the tubs was so dry that it was impossible to soak it and to revive the plants, so another disaster faced us and we had to replant at the end of the season. During that summer we kept the tubs going by taking over plants in flower from the nursery, plunging them in the soil, taking the plants off their canes and tying them to the twilmesh panels. At the end of the season several people remarked on how beautiful the clematis had been all summer, little realising that they had been changed every week, which just goes to prove how easy it is to fool most of the people most of the time.

Since then the tubs have been replaced with large plastic pots and, as the concert season has been extended throughout the summer, we have planted them with 'Jackmanii' varieties which flower non-stop

73

throughout the summer months. These are pruned hard in February every year, and while they are growing we adopt the method we used when they dried out in that hot summer. We force plants for the Chelsea Flower Show early in the year and usually have several to spare, so we take them over to the Maltings to fill up the empty frames for the Easter concerts and the June festival.

Exhibiting at local shows, our clematis became well known and I was soon asked to speak at garden society meetings, Women's Institutes, etc. The first was at Lowestoft and this was before I had a camera or a car, and so some kind lady came to fetch me and bring me home again. All I had to help me were a few specimens, a graft, a few cuttings and some early flowers to hand round while I was talking. I was terrified to see all those faces looking back at me, whichever way I turned. It was only the advice I was given before the lecture that kept me going. A friend had told me to look round the audience and say to myself, 'What an ignorant lot they are, none of them know anything about clematis.' So, filled with an uneasy self-confidence, I struggled through and enjoyed answering many questions at the end.

After that I bought a ciné camera and a 35-mm one for taking stills, and we made a film of all that goes on in the nursery, fancying ourselves as film stars, from the early part of the year when we start grafting, through cutting time in the early summer, potting up all the many plants, packing and sending them out during the autumn, planting and pruning, and finally some shots of different varieties and a few shots of our exhibit at Chelsea, which all made quite an interesting film. I also took several slides of various varieties and so was able to show this film and the slides and talk in the darkness while everyone was looking at the screen and not at me, which was much easier and is an ideal way, for the nervous, of giving a lecture. It is surprising how bold one becomes, however, after a few lectures.

By now we had left the 'bicycle' age behind; I had passed my driving test and acquired a car, and I was soon going all over the place in the winter giving lectures throughout East Anglia and beyond. The furthest afield I went was to Leicester which, to me, having lived and worked in Leicester for four years before the war, was a great thrill. A garden society at Cambridge wanted me to lecture there about the same time and so I stayed the night in Leicester with friends, and, on the way home, called at Cambridge and gave my lecture there – what a great thrill to say one has lectured at Cambridge! These lectures began to take up too much time, however, and so, towards the end of the 1960s, I gave them up completely. We still send our slides to garden societies, together with typewritten notes that can be read while slides are being shown and so we are able to lecture by proxy even further afield. The personal touch is lost, of course, but for most societies this is a much cheaper method as we only charge the cost of postage. We now have several sets of slides and send them all over the British Isles; we have even sent them abroad as far as Argentina!

'H. F. Young' flowers in May and June to give this magnificent display.

The local BBC arrived one day to make a film of the nursery and to interview me, which was another terrifying experience. The whole day was taken up in preparing what was, in the end, a ten-minute film. Cameramen, sound engineers, lighting engineers, the interviewer and the producer were all over the place, and masses of wire covered our lawn. I sat with the interviewer in our walled garden on a low brick wall with a microphone clipped to my jacket and chatted about the nursery before the cameras rolled. The producer said, 'That's fine, now let's have it for real,' and of course I dried up and the first take was a disaster, as were the second and third. Eventually they got something out of it and after I had walked up and down the pergola to introduce the programme, they left, leaving me feeling like a limp rag. Since then I have had the greatest sympathy for anyone being interviewed on TV. They eventually rang me up about six months later and said, 'Your programme is on tonight after the six o'clock news.' No time to let anyone know, which was perhaps just as well, but several customers who came in during the weeks that followed said, 'We saw you on TV.' So it did a little good.

We have sent clematis to many different countries – Canada, the USA, Bermuda, Argentina, Chile, Mexico, to most countries of Europe and to South Africa, Australia, New Zealand, Hong Kong and Japan. Most orders have come through contacts at Chelsea, but British garden papers seem to travel the world and we are always being asked to send our catalogues to distant countries. Packing for dispatch abroad presents a problem, as in most countries no soil is allowed to be sent with the plant. This means that plants can only be sent in our autumn, which means that clematis sent to the Southern Hemisphere get a very quick winter – they are sent by air and so their winter usually lasts the duration of the flight! They do not seem to miss their dormant season, however, and start growing directly they arrive.

Some countries are extremely fussy and every speck of soil must be washed off the roots. They have to be inspected, before they are packed, by an official from the Ministry of Agriculture. The chief culprit he or she is looking for is eelworm, a minute creature that cannot be seen with the naked eye, but which leaves tell-tale cysts on the roots and causes havoc in countries with a warmer climate than Britain. When we grew clematis in loam imported from various parts of the UK, we had several consignments rejected, but now that we grow all our plants in Levington compost the risk no longer exists and our roots are beautifully strong and clean.

Once they had been examined the inspector sent off a report to the Ministry of Agriculture and they sent us a health certificate which went with the plants along with their import licence. Each plant was wrapped tightly in a polythene bag which kept the roots moist during its journey. They were sent in long cardboard boxes, packed in wood wool and arrived at their destination in perfect condition.

We have had many letters of thanks and photographs of the plants in flower from people overseas. We keep in touch with some customers, exchanging ideas and news of success or otherwise of their plants. Often new plants were exchanged and we have had several varieties from Canada, Argentina and Poland.

We have now stopped sending plants abroad as the Ministry of Agriculture have introduced a charge for inspecting such plants, and we thought it was rather too high to pass on to our customers. As I did the exporting completely on my own, but am now retired, I thought it was time to pack it in and devote more time to looking after Chelsea plants and established plants on our walls, pergolas, etc., in the nursery, which get sadly neglected as there is so much to do in a nursery growing several thousand clematis.

Sending packed plants throughout the British Isles is a much simpler method as they can be sent with the soil still on the roots; in fact still in their pots, or in a paper one which is exchanged for the plastic one at the time of packing. They are sent mostly by post. One box, in which we can put one or two plants, is 2 ft (60 cm) by 4½ in (10 cm) by 4½ in. The canes are cut down to 2 ft (60 cm) to fit the

'Henryi', also known as 'Bangholme Belle'. A good strong and vigorous variety from the 19th century.

box, there being no necessity to send a long cane. With two plants, we put a pot, wrapped in a polythene bag, at either end and fix a cardboard strip above and below the cane to stop the pots moving about in the box. Wood wool is packed round the pots, planting instructions are enclosed, the top of the box is stapled to the bottom and off they go.

The larger-sized box, 2 ft (60 cm) by 9 in (23 cm) by 4½ in (10 cm), holds four or six plants and is reinforced by bamboo canes across the middle of the box. As long as they are not thrown about too much they arrive in perfect condition. For a dozen plants or more, clematis are sent by road transport, standing upright in a wooden box with stakes at each corner which are brought together over the tops of the plants, tied and topped with wood wool, to look like a wigwam in a box. This is the ideal method of sending them, but far too costly for a smaller number of plants.

Clematis growers have been sending plants out on long canes for a hundred years now and so, naturally, the public expect a clematis with a long thin stem tied to a cane, but of course it is only the root that need be sent. The plant could be cut down to the lowest pair of buds and packed in a small square box, or, for several plants, in a box with sections to fit each pot. After all, we usually advise people to cut down their plant, the first spring after planting, to the lowest pair of buds (and the hard-pruning ones must be pruned hard every year). So why not send them out in the autumn already cut down? One day some brave nurseryman will try this out, and after the first few years of complaints from irate customers, and after he has gone bankrupt, the idea will catch on and in 50 years' time all clematis will be sent this way.

Most plants sent out nowadays are one year old, or in their second season, and thus often called two-year plants and of course this method of cutting down to the lowest pair of buds before packing is ideal for them, as they will often shoot up with two shoots the following season.

I should like to see advertised in clematis catalogues plants that have been in the nursery for two or three years, have been cut down every winter and made strong bushy plants with two or three stems. There are many containers that can be used for such plants, but of course the drawback is time and space. To hold a plant back in the nursery to grow on into an older plant is almost impossible, especially when stock is running low at the end of the season. It is always a great temptation to send them out rather than disappoint a customer. Older plants would grow outside, of course, and so need no green-house space, but one would need a fair amount of ground space to stand these plants on and would need to give them a good deal of attention to try to keep them on their own canes and prevent them strangling each other. So the cost of these plants would be high, but it would be well worth while to get a ready-made plant. A small one-year plant has to face the rigours of its first winter, often straight out of a greenhouse, albeit a cold one. It is surprising the number that do survive, which goes to prove how tough and hardy clematis really are.

In one of our early catalogues we offered collections of clematis, that is, a collection of four plants for spring flowering, four for summer flowering, six to give a continuation of bloom from May to October, etc. These were offered at a reduced rate and were sent carriage paid. These collections were named after our local areas, 'The Suffolk Collection', 'The East Anglian Collection' and the 'Minsmere Collection'. This last one was named after the world-famous bird sanctuary which is situated within our village of Westleton. We sent this collection to the Royal Society for the Protection of Birds (RSPB) at Sandy, Bedfordshire and as far as I know it is still growing well.

Our most popular collection has undoubtedly been 'The Beginner's Collection'. This was suggested to me by Philip Holmes who was working for me at the time. He is now a celebrity in his own right as a fisherman on the beach at our local seaside village of Dunwich where he regales visitors with tales of the lost city of Dunwich and church bells which can be heard ringing in rough weather from the churches under the sea! He said, 'Why don't you give them a collec-

*C. integrifolia* 'Durandii'. Most clematis climb by using their leaves, but this one needs tying to its support.

tion of three or four tough hardy varieties that anyone can grow,' so the Beginner's Collection came into existence. These collections have now been abandoned as it seems that these days customers prefer to make their own selection, but in the early years of the nursery they were very popular.

Dodger, as Philip Holmes is affectionately known, became quite a star attraction at the Chelsea Flower Show where the ladies loved his bluff country style of talking. I shall never forget the time when a lady asked him what to do about her clematis that wouldn't grow. Dodger replied in his broad Suffolk voice, 'What you want to do, ma'am, is to put some muck on it.' On another occasion in the nursery a lady was buying a 250-ft (76 m) reel of wire to wire up her wall to support clematis. She asked Dodger how far it would go and Dodger, with a huge grin, replied, 'Two hundred and fifty feet, ma'am', which was not quite what the lady meant.

Many of our customers have had a go at raising clematis from seed

– a long process, as clematis seed take two or three years to germinate, but the results may well be worth waiting for. Miss Kathleen Dunford of Hampshire sowed some seed in a pot and nothing came up, so the pot was put under the greenhouse bench and a year later a seedling was found growing which developed into a striking rosy-pink semi-double. It now bears her name and is found in most catalogues throughout the world. I tried a cutting of this variety which Miss Dunford sent through the post, but cuttings from outside plants are difficult to strike and we had no luck. We tried hard wood grafts in the spring, still without success, and finally I had to go down to her delightful cottage in the New Forest and layer the original plant itself, returning the following year to dig the plants up and take them back to Suffolk as stock plants. Before I arrived to do the layering Miss Dunford's sister said, 'I wonder if Mr Fisk has brought everything necessary for layering,' and Kathleen Dunford replied, 'I bet he hasn't.' And neither had I! Still, they were good gardeners and we soon found pots to sink round the plant, John Innes compost to fill the pots, wires to peg down the layers and stones to hold them down. When I went back for them the following year they had been well looked after and the pots were full of roots.

We have introduced several new clematis but the best one was 'Dr Ruppel' from Argentina. We sent the real Dr Ruppel a plant of 'Capitan Thuilleaux', saying it was an improved 'Bees Jubilee', which is an improved 'Nelly Moser'. The following year he wrote saying that he had an even better variety and would send me a plant. This eventually arrived in the middle of the summer and looked completely dead until we realised that it was winter time in Argentina. So we potted up 'Dr Ruppel' and in a few weeks it was shooting nicely and we were able to take a few cuttings and increase it still further, finding out what an excellent variety it is. Since then it has been exported all over the world and from this one small dead-looking plant thousands of 'Dr Ruppels' have been raised and in very many gardens this magnificent variety is loved and greatly admired.

Another variety that is becoming very popular, which we have had the privilege of introducing, is 'Louise Rowe'. This is a double lilac-mauve with wavy sepals and golden stamens. The great attraction of this variety, a cross between 'Lasurstern' and 'William Kennett,' is the fact that it flowers in May and June with double, semi-double and single flowers all at the same time! Mrs Rowe, who named it after a member of her family, tells me she is very keen on hybridising; she says that she 'rubs their noses together' at the appropriate time. Her first result is certainly a winner and there are more to come.

We have little time in the nursery for hybridising and too little space, as there are usually hundreds of plants thrown away before there is one worth keeping, but we have dabbled in it and so far have produced three new varieties – 'Alice Fisk' was raised in 1964, and is a cross between 'Lasurstern' and 'Mrs Cholmondeley', having the

'Jackmanii', the oldest of the hybrids was raised in 1860 at Jackman's Nursery in Surrey and has been going strong ever since.

colour of 'Mrs Cholmondeley' and the shape of 'Lasurstern'. It is named after my mother who was almost 80 at the time. She spent a great deal of time in the nursery, weeding, tying up plants, getting plants ready for shows and many other jobs that were an enormous help to us. She loved every minute of it and her life was full of interest and meaning. My mother could frighten the living daylights out of anyone with a look that became known as 'Granny's look'. We used to put the 'closed' sign out at 5 p.m. during the summer and woe betide any customer who ignored it. Mother's ferocious glare and her 'Can't you read?' would frighten off the most persistent customer, and many a time I have seen someone slinking out of the nursery almost with their tail between their legs!

It was a great thrill for her when we published our catalogue in 1967 with her clematis on the front cover. She worked every day in the nursery until a stroke in August 1970, and she died the following month at the age of 87. Needless to say she had masses of clematis at her funeral, including her own 'Alice Fisk'.

The other varieties raised in the nursery are named after my two secretaries who have been such a great help to me in the office for several years. 'Gladys Picard' is a beautiful delicate mauve-pink clematis tinged with deeper pink, a strong and vigorous grower.

'Gillian Blades', who was my first secretary, Gillian Alexander, is a star-shaped pure white clematis with crenulated edges and is a very free-flowering variety. In the 1950s I was in touch with a clematis grower in Sweden who used to send us transparencies and flowers, and one day he sent me some flowers and promised us a plant of a yellow clematis. This was quite exciting as there had been no such thing as a yellow clematis. It arrived in the autumn, a sturdy young plant, and we kept it safely through the winter. The following spring we forced it on to provide grafts and cuttings, but the growth it sent out was weak and feeble and we were not very successful. During the following summer Tage Lundell's account of trials with it in his garden were not very encouraging and so we did not persevere with it, which was one of the biggest boobs we ever made, for a few years later Treasures of Tenbury Wells introduced it at Chelsea as the first yellow clematis and called it 'Yellow Queen', not a very good name as the colour is a pale primrose and after a few days in flower it turns white.

I did not know at the time that this was the same plant from Tage Lundell in Sweden, and as we had had our plants for some years, I thought we might as well have a yellow one in our catalogue as well. Our facilities had greatly improved by then and we were more successful with cuttings. We named our plant 'Moonlight' and included it in our catalogue a year or two later. At the next Chelsea I was talking to Raymond Evison on Treasures' stand at Chelsea (all clematis growers are a very friendly lot and we often exchange ideas and suggestions and help each other out with plants), and I mentioned that his 'Yellow Queen' looked very much like our 'Moonlight' and asked where his came from. He said from Sweden where they had a customer who was very keen on hybridising clematis and I said, 'Tage Lundell?' Raymond looked rather surprised and said, 'Yes, do you know him as well?' So 'Yellow Queen' and 'Moonlight' are one and the same plant, but I still think it is a poor grower and not a very good colour. Maybe one day someone will be able to cross this variety with another clematis and get a clearer yellow, although, personally speaking, I am not too keen on a bright yellow clematis; like the pink daffodil and yellow lilac it will never be very popular.

In 1974 I took into partnership with me Edward Collett, a young man who had worked in the nursery since he left shcool – in fact, even before leaving school, as many of the young lads of the village do in their turn, coming up on Saturday mornings and during school holidays to earn some holiday money. Teddy, as he is affectionately called, was always more interested in clematis than most other boys and he was one of our best salesmen at the several Chelsea Flower Shows we attended. In 1968 he was looking round the village for a plot on which to build a bungalow when he got married. His search was in vain so I offered him a piece of land at the nursery, which had never been much used. With the help of most of the young lads of the village and a few tradesmen, he built his own bungalow, a wonderful

'Jackmanii Superba'.
The sepals of this
variety are broader
than those of
'Jackmanii'.

'Jackmanii Alba'.
Bluish-white double
flowers appear first,
followed by pure
white single flowers
all summer long. (*far
right*)

'Jackmanii'. A close-
up of this very
popular variety.
(*right*)

83

and praiseworthy achievement, and he now lives at the nursery. Having no heir myself, my brother living at this time in Malvern and having only two daughters, it occurred to me that it would be a good idea to make Teddy my heir. So I told him that if he liked I would take him into partnership when I retired, or when the firm had reached a good business footing, whichever was the sooner. The latter was the sooner and so we are now in partnership and working well together.

In the meantime my brother Jack at Malvern had lost his wife and had remarried, and he suggested that they should come back home and help in the nursery, which they did. His trade is carpentry, so he has been most useful in building greenhouses and in general repairs. As a sideline he grows fuchsias. He has become quite expert at it and sells his plants in the plantaria in the nursery.

The present generation of the Fisk family had so far had no boys, only girls, and we all thought that the name would eventually die out – I have constantly been told that it was up to me to keep the line going, but I am a confirmed bachelor! Fortunately, however, my brother and his wife Sheila decided to start another family and, much to our great delight, they now have two boys, John and James, to carry on the name of the Fisk family who have lived in Westleton for hundreds of years. My brother and I were christened Jack and Jim, so now we have put matters right by christening the two boys John and James, which may lead to complications with four J. Fisks living in the same house! When my partnership with Teddy was approaching, I suggested to my brother that he should take over the wholesale side of the business, and he and his wife now run this, leaving Teddy and me to run the retail side of things, a happy solution which seems to be working well.

The nursery itself is very small, but as we are known worldwide people always expect to find a place of several acres when they arrive. Actually we are less than 1 acre (4,000 sq m), but plants in pots do not take up much room and so we can grow several thousand on a small plot. Most of the land is covered by greenhouses and polythene tunnel houses, so there are quite a number of places for the public to look round and walk through. All the houses are open for viewing, so, although we are small in size, there is plenty to see as well as the walled garden and pergola.

There are usually plants on sale the whole year round, although in the winter some varieties are in short supply. From late spring onwards, however, everything is available, or almost everything, as there are always those awkward varieties that are difficult to propagate, or are in great demand owing to publicity in garden articles in the press or on TV programmes. We often try to anticipate these demands, of course, but it is very difficult and one can soon find oneself landed with too many of certain varieties.

Anglia Television ran a series of half-hour village programmes in the 1970s and Westleton was chosen as one of the subjects. We have a large car-park and the TV crew asked if they could park their lorries

'John Warren',
growing in an
Australian garden.

and lift here for the two days while they were recording in the village, so, naturally, they also chose the nursery as one of the items featured! There was great excitement in the village as the cameras went round filming. It finally came to our turn and I was interviewed standing in front of a lych gate covered with pink *montana*s. This time I wasn't quite so frightened of the cameras. It was fortunate that they came to film the village in May as everywhere they went there were pink and white *montana*s covering houses, fences and trees. Someone said to me when it was eventually shown on the box, 'That was a good advert you had on TV the other day Jim!' And it was too.

We were also on TV a little later on when the Pope came to Britain, not that there was any real connection, but indirectly there was. One of my Polish customers was a Jesuit monk, Brother Stefan Franczak, and he had sent me, the previous year, two plants of a clematis he had raised and named after Jan Pawel II (John Paul II). His Holiness had also accepted a plant to grow in the Vatican. We potted them up in preparation for propagating the following spring. Early that year the BBC rang us and asked if we would take part in the programme that goes out just before the Chelsea Flower Show, called *Growing for Gold*. We naturally said 'yes' and they said, 'Have you got any new varieties that we could come up and film?' and I said 'Well, we've got two plants of a new clematis named after the Pope but that is all.'

'Splendid,' they said, 'that's just what we want, especially as he is visiting Britain about the same time as Chelsea. When will it be in flower?'

I protested that we only had two plants and hadn't had a chance to propagate any at all, but they brushed aside my argument and told me to 'phone up when it was in bloom. Fortunately they were two fine plants with a few good buds on them and when one looked like flowering I rang them up and the film crew arrived with Peter

Seabrook and spent the day filming in the nursery for what was another ten-minute spot on the programme. I had written to Brother Franczak to tell him about this and he got in touch with a Polish friend of his in Luton, Mr Bestjan, and between them they arranged for Brother Franczak to be flown over from Poland to appear on the programme standing in front of our stand at Chelsea.

We saved our second plant for Chelsea, as it had four splendid buds on it, although we sacrificed one bud to cut off the shoot to provide grafting wood in March, leaving three buds on for Chelsea. Just before the show two of these buds wilted leaving just one to go up to the show, but this came out too soon and by the time it got up to the show it had lost its colour, a lovely cream with pink trails, and was almost white. Still, it survived the visit of the cameras, with Brother Franczak standing beside it. Half-way through the week, in tidying up the exhibit before the show opened, I accidentally knocked off two of the sepals, so we had to finish Chelsea with a photograph which Lawrence Vulliamy, the director of the programme, had taken when he visited the nursery a few weeks previously!

'Jan Pawel II' (John Paul II) is a good grower but has one bad fault; the pink trails in the flower develop into a pink bar in late summer and early autumn and then it looks for all the world like 'Nelly Moser'. We have had several calls from irate customers who accused us of sending them a 'Nelly Moser'. We assure them that it is a true 'John Paul II' and if they leave it unpruned they will get the flower pictured in the catalogue. Obviously 'Nelly Moser' is one of the parents. Brother Franczak is very good at hybridising and has sent us several good varieties. Three of the best are 'Kardynal Wyszynski', a summer-flowering cardinal red, 'Kacper', a superb early-flowering violet, and 'Warszawska Nike' (pronounced 'neekay'), a very good late velvet-purple.

We do very little advertising nowadays, the Chelsea Flower Show is our main advertisement and we usually sell around 7,000 catalogues there during the week. Most of them are bought for reference, of course, as it is more than just a list of varieties. We try to put in as much information as possible about pruning, planting, growing and even clematis wilt. We often get written about in magazines and newspapers, which is a wonderful free advertisement. Michael Barrett of *Gardeners News* paid us a visit one hot summer and, finding it rather untidy, was delighted to find handwritten notices around the nursery apologising for the weeds. He wrote,

> Faced not only by lack of rain but also by other problems, he has scattered handwritten placards around the place which say things like this: 'Our apologies for weeds and untidyness in some of the tunnel houses but we have just been to the Chelsea Flower Show and the Suffolk Show, and at the moment we are busy packing and taking cuttings. We hope to have the nursery clean and tidy within a week or two.

He went on to say that he thought this was refreshingly honest and so

'Lady Northcliffe'.
An ideal variety for
the small garden.

was the catalogue for, as he puts is, 'Although it naturally refers in the most glowing terms to "The Queen of Climbers" it devotes a whole page to that scourge of the species, clematis wilt.' And he headed his article 'Jim'll fix it'!

Another amusing article appeared in *The Sunday Times*, written by Graham Rose. He thought that, 'It must be the fascination with rigging that attracts sailors to clematis', and went on to say,

> I like to think that Jim Fisk, one of Britain's premier clematis growers, and his partner Edward Collett are both men of the sea. Fisk himself served in the Navy during the War and instinctively chose clematis when he set up his Nursery in 1950. And Collett who remains a keen amateur sailor, had been destined for the Lowestoft fishing fleet, when at the age of 16, he asked Fisk for a temporary job 'until I find a ship'. It is easy to understand why he found clematis more alluring than mermaids. Not even in the most rum-soaked of imaginations can the sea-nymphs match the real life beauty and variety of the clematis world – a fact which Fisk complains is too little appreciated.

We are always grateful for these free write-ups, particularly if they mention the price of the catalogue, a very expensive item these days, especially as it is illustrated in colour.

In 1985 we enlarged the nursery for the first time in 30 years, and bought about a quarter of an acre (1,000 sq m) of land in the field next door. This ran behind one of our neighbours' large garden and, being on friendly terms with them, we told them about it, just in case! They were quite happy about it, however, until they arrived home from a holiday in Tenerife the following March. Freda went up to her bedroom, looked out of the window and was horrified to see a large 60-ft (18 m) tunnel house going the whole length of the bottom of her garden, on the other side of her hedge of course. Immediately the 'phone rang and I was summoned next door! This was the day of the big gale of that year and I went round full of apologies to assure them that when the leaves appeared on their high hedge they wouldn't see it. So we took a walk down the garden with the wind howling round our ears and I laughingly joked that, 'Perhaps this wind will blow it away,' and an hour later it had! When we put it up again we offered to colour it green and Rusty bought some big conifers to fill up a few gaps and all was well. Two years later, in the hurricane of 1987, we lost three tunnel houses and a large 50-ft (15 m) glasshouse full of cuttings for the following year's crop. We managed to save most of them, but it just goes to show how vulnerable nurseries and market gardens are when nature gets out of hand.

We seem to have settled into a routine nowadays, in fact the nursery almost runs itself. The early part of the year is taken up with maintenance and having a good clean up. Then, in January, plants are brought in to a warm greenhouse to force them on to provide early cuttings. In February we take hardwood cuttings of the *montana* varieties. In March and April we take an early batch of cuttings and the main batch of cuttings are taken in May and June, just at Chelsea time, which used to be very awkward until we discovered the method of covering the trays and cuttings with polythene so that there is no need to spray and water for two weeks, when the polythene is removed, dried, turned over and replaced for another two weeks. So we can now go away for two weeks without worrying. Packing is done in the autumn nowadays as sending plants out in the spring coincides with our busiest time and, as they have started growing, they are liable to get damaged. In the autumn they are dormant and travel very well although we do get the occasional letter complaining that we have sent dead plants! We explain that the plants are dormant and will shoot out all right in the spring and that we will replace them if they don't. Needless to say we never hear any more, so there is another satisfied customer.

We seem to have very happy relations with our customers, or most of them anyway; we have our usual quota of difficult ones as most businesses seem to do! The secret of good relations is, of course, the personal touch, which we have managed to keep, and to follow the advice I was given by a customer when I first started. I was proudly showing him round one day and, as he left, he turned to me and said, 'Whatever you do, don't get too big.' I have tried to follow his advice and, although we are known all over the world and have been to shows all over the country, we have managed to remain a small business and to retain in the nursery that happy atmosphere, which, when everything went well on board when I was in the navy, was referred to as a 'happy ship'.

88

## · 10 ·
# QUESTIONS
# WE ARE ASKED

e are asked some extraordinary things during the course of the year. We are frequently asking, when we put the 'closed' notice up at five o'clock, 'Are you really closed?' We were also asked once in the middle of a mild January, 'Why haven't you sent my plants; you promised them in the spring?' In the main, however, we get asked sensible questions and this chapter gives a selection of some of the more interesting ones. They are not in any special order, just a hotchpotch of whys, hows and whats! However, they may answer your particular question, save you a stamp in writing to the nursery and save us time, paper and another stamp in reply! Here goes then:

*My clematis looks dead at the bottom and all the leaves are brown. Is it dying?*
No, your clematis is alive and well and is probably flowering quite happily at the top. The dead leaves are simply those first early leaves that have done their job and are now naturally dying. Plenty of water and good feeding will keep them green a little longer, but with certain plants, especially the pink and red varieties, this happens every summer. The dead leaves can be cut off or you could grow something in front to hide them.

*Do clematis need a limy soil?*
No, this is a fallacy that has grown up over the years since it was first realised that our native clematis only grows on chalky soils. Clematis will grow in practically any soil so long as they are provided with plenty of water and plenty of nutrients in the form of a top-dressing of manure in the autumn and a good soaking once a week with a general liquid fertiliser during the growing season, especially where the soils are hot, dry and hungry.

*Can two clematis be grown in the same spot?*
Yes, two varieties of contrasting colour look most effective, but make sure that they are both of the same pruning habit; in the spring 'Nelly Moser' and 'Lasurstern' look well together, also 'Henryi' and 'William

Kennett'. A good summer-flowering pair would be 'Jackmanii' and 'Madame Edouard André' or 'Perle d'Azur' and 'Comtesse de Bouchaud', and in the autumn 'Rouge Cardinal' and 'Gipsy Queen'.

*Will clematis grow in the north of Scotland?*
Of course they will. Clematis are extremely hardy in spite of their exotic-looking appearance. They grow well in Norway and Sweden and so should be quite happy anywhere in the British Isles.

*My clematis has been in over a year and hasn't moved yet, what can I do?*
Some varieties will stand still for a complete season, but there is nothing to worry about. As soon as the roots have established themselves the plant will grow. You can help it by giving it a good soaking of any general fertiliser every week during the growing season.

*My plant has grown well this year but has not produced a single flower. Why is this?*
In some seasons a plant will go 'blind' for no apparent reason. Those varieties that flower in the summer can sometimes be persuaded to bloom by cutting back the young wood about half-way. This will encourage side shoots to break which will flower later in the season. Regular feeding with a fertiliser which has a high potash content will help, such as sulphate of potash.

*My flowers are green this year, how should I treat them?*
A handful of sulphate of potash will soon remedy this. The early-flowering varieties such as 'Nelly Moser', 'Barbara Dibley', 'Lasurstern' and 'Mrs Cholmondeley' are the worst offenders, but if you have been feeding regularly then your flowers should never go green.

*Are there any scented clematis?*
Yes, *C. armandii* and most of the *montanas* are scented, especially *C. montana* 'Elizabeth' and *C. montana* 'Wilsonii'. The other *montanas* have scent in varying degrees. Later-flowering varieties, such as *C. davidiana*, *C. flammula*, *C. rehderiana* and *C. recta* all have strong perfumes. Only one of the large flowering hybrids has any scent. This is 'Fair Rosamond' which has the delicate perfume of violets.

*Will clematis grow indoors?*
Not very successfully; they are essentially a plant of the open air and to try to keep them indoors is difficult and almost impossible. What you could do would be to grow them in tubs outside, and then, just as the flowers start to open, bring them indoors for as long as the flowers last, standing them outside for the winter and covering the tubs with polythene or sacking in extreme frosts only.

*C. macropetala*, one of the loveliest of the species, flowering in April and May. (*above*)

*C. macropetala* 'Markhamii'. The pink version of *C. macropetala*. (*above, top right*)

*C. macropetala* 'White Swan'. One of the several white varieties of *C. macropetala*. (*above, bottom right*)

*C. macropetala* 'Maidwell Hall', also known as 'Blue Lagoon', growing here with *C. alpina* 'White Moth'.

*Can I move a well-established plant?*
Yes, but the plant will probably sulk for the following year. The best time to move them is in November. They will have settled in by the following spring, but from then on keep them well watered and fed with liquid manure.

*I have a small walled garden with 6-ft-high (2 m) walls. What varieties can I grow?*
There are several varieties that do not grow much above 6 ft (2 m) and can be easily trained to fit this height. They are *C. alpina*, *C. macropetala*, 'Alice Fisk', 'Barbara Dibley', 'Barbara Jackman', 'Comtesse de Bouchaud', 'Hagley Hybrid', 'Haku Ookan', 'Lady Northcliffe', 'Madame Edouard André', 'Maureen', 'Miss Bateman', 'Mrs N. Thompson', 'Prince Charles', *C. texensis* 'Gravetye Beauty', 'The President', 'Xerxes'.

*My evergreen* C. calycina *has never bloomed. It has been in three years, will it ever flower?*
This variety does take some time to establish itself, but it should be flowering in its third or fourth year. A high potash fertiliser will help.

*My plant looked dead on arrival this autumn; is it all right?*
Most clematis are deciduous and in the autumn many will have lost their leaves and consequently look dead. It is alive and will be shooting into new growth in the spring.

*The flowers on my clematis are getting smaller every year. How can I get them back to their normal size?*
Clematis produce a thick mass of roots, and in time the ground below becomes very dry as well as losing its goodness. This is usually the cause of small flowers. Drive a pipe down to below the roots in the spring and pour several gallons of water down to soak the bone-dry soil. Keep it well watered during the summer and give a good soak of a liquid fertiliser every week. Your flowers will soon resume their normal size.

*Are there any clematis that will grow on north-facing walls?*
Several. The best ones are the *alpina*, *macropetala* and *montana* varieties, and, amongst the large-flowering hybrids, the following varieties: 'Comtesse de Bouchaud', 'Henryi', 'Jackmanii', 'Marie Boisellot', 'Mrs Cholmondeley', 'Nelly Moser', 'Victoria' and 'William Kennett'.

*Can clematis be grown in tubs?*
Certainly, provided the tub is large enough. Clematis roots go down 2 ft (60 cm) or more in the garden, so a deep tub or large pot is essential – at least 18 in (45 cm). Some good soil must also be used, such as John Innes No. 3, and good drainage provided at the bottom of the tub, with some well-rotted manure placed over the top of the drain-

*C. montana* growing in its natural habitat in Nepal. (*top*)

*C. montana* growing 60 ft (18 m) high in pine trees. (*top, right*)

*C. montana* 'Mayleen'. A good pink variety, beautifully scented. (*top, far right*)

*C. montana* 'Pink Perfection'. A wall of scented pink blossoms.

*C. montana* 'Wilsonii'. A late flowering variety, strongly scented. Seen growing at Snape Maltings, the home of the Aldeburgh Festival. (*bottom, right*)

*C. montana tetrarose*, the largest of the *montanas*. (*bottom, far right*)

age. Clematis in tubs must be kept moist at all times; once a tub has dried out it is difficult to get it moist again, except by soaking it in a tank of water. Regular feeding must also be the rule, as the roots are naturally restricted. Feed at least once a week, twice if possible, with a general liquid fertiliser.

*My plant is in a hopeless tangle. What can I do?*
In this case it is best to cut it down to the ground, or back to the old wood if it is a *montana* or a very old hybrid variety. This can be done quite safely during the winter. It can then be trained properly during the following season.

*Are clematis any good as cut flowers?*
Yes, but some varieties will not hold up very long. They can be revived by floating them in deep water during the night. Some of the large-flowering hybrids will keep in water for up to three weeks. Experiments will soon find out which are the best varieties. One attractive method is to float a number of flower-heads in a large flat bowl; even one in a saucer with foliage makes an unusual table decoration.

*How long do clematis live?*
There are some records of the variety 'Jackmanii' living for over 50 years. The *montana* varieties will live for much longer than that. Some of the *montanas* planted by William Robinson at Gravetye Manor in Sussex, where there was once a famous clematis garden, are still going strong, and in his book on how he made the garden in 1893 there is an entry 'Planted montanas'.

*Are there any evergreen clematis?*
Yes, the best one being *C. armandii*, which is the hardiest of several large-leaved evergreens; most of the other varieties are not hardy in Britain. Two very hardy varieties are the small-leaved *C. calycina* and *C. cirrhosa*.

*Why does my clematis only bloom at the top?*
*Why can't I get my clematis to bloom low down?*
These two questions are linked, as clematis that only flower at the top are the 'Jackmanii' varieties. These flower only on the young wood and must make a certain amount of growth before they flower, so they will never bloom at the base of the plant. If you want plants that will bloom closer to the ground, then you must choose early-flowering varieties.

*Should I remove the seedheads after flowering?*
For the first year, yes. But after that they can be left on the plant. They can make very effective indoor decorations for the winter.

94

A hedge of clematis. 'Margaret Hunt' (pink), 'Madame Edouard André' (red), and 'Jackmanii' (purple).

*How far apart should clematis be planted?*
A general answer would be 5 ft (1.5 m), but it all depends on the variety. The *montanas*, for instance, will cover 30 ft (9 m) or more, and varieties such as 'Hagley Hybrid' and 'Madame Edouard André' only make plants 2–3 ft (60–120 cm) across.

*My plant is covered with a grey mould. What is it and what is the cure?*
This is mildew, which, in certain seasons, attacks some of the 'Jackmanii' varieties, notably the red ones. The attack is fortunately not carried from one year to the next. At the first signs, usually at the end of June, spray with Karathene and repeat at intervals as necessary or dust with green sulphur.

*Why are the leaves of my evergreen* C. armandii *going brown?*
These are the old leaves, for although a plant is termed an evergreen, this does not mean that its leaves last for ever. New leaves are produced every year and the old ones go brown, die and fall off. New growth will eventually cover the dead and dying leaves. Wind can cause damage to young leaves, however, by bruising them against a wall for instance and making them go brown.

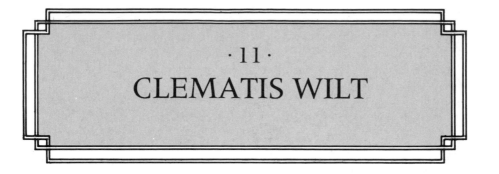

## ·11·
# CLEMATIS WILT

n the book *Clematis as a Garden Flower* by Thomas Moore and George Jackman, published in 1877, there is no mention of the word wilt! Was there no such thing as clematis wilt in those days? It seems that such was the case, judging from their enormous popularity a hundred years ago. Since then, however, wilt has become a word to strike terror into the hearts of all clematis devotees. Did clematis wilt exist one hundred years ago? Or was it hushed up in the catalogues and in Jackman and Moore's book? If not, when did it start?

It was prevalent in the early 1900s, as William Robinson, writing on clematis, accused nurserymen of bringing wilt into clematis by the practice of grafting. This has since been proved to be quite wrong, as when clematis are grafted, as he himself found out later on, the stock is only used as a nurse-stock; by the time the clematis are planted out into the garden the scion has produced its own roots and the stock is discarded. The modern method of producing clematis in most nurseries these days is by cuttings, and these have wilted just as easily as grafted plants.

A gleam of hope has emerged, however, with the introduction of Benlate, a fungicide which seems to exercise a certain control over clematis wilt, as one of my customers remarked in his letter, 'Benlate than never'. Gardeners would be well advised to spray the base of their plants with Benlate in the autumn, again in the spring and once a month during the summer.

It seems to be at the base of the plants where this attack takes place. When wilt occurs it is as though the plant has been cut through with a knife or hoe. Everything above this spot hangs limply and it is especially infuriating when the plant is in full bud or bloom and was apparently healthy. The only thing that can be done when this happens is to cut the plant right down to the ground. It is no good watering and spraying, the damage has been done and all that remains is to remove the wilted stems and foliage and burn them. Provided the clematis has been planted deeply as suggested on page 27, there is every chance of shoots soon coming up from the buried first pair of nodes. Water and feed well to encourage these nodes to develop.

Many theories have been advanced as to the cause of clematis wilt. Ernest Markham, in his book *Clematis,* even has a name for the fungus that is supposed to be the cause of the disease. He says, 'In 1915 a Bulletin was published which dealt with *Ascochyta clematindina,* as this fatal disease is named. The Bulletin was written by Mr W. O. Gloyer and published by the New York Agricultural Experimental Station in Geneva, New York, USA.'

The action of the fungus was described as follows:
The plants are killed by the growth of the fungus down the petiole into the stems, thus girdling the plant at the node. The stem may be girdled also by the lesions anywhere in the internodes. Dead stubs left on the vines are a means of holding the disease over a period of time. New shoots may be formed below the girdled region, but the downward progress of the fungus ultimately kills the plant if the diseased tissue is not removed.

He goes on to say that various spraying experiments were carried out, such as dusting with sulphur, spraying with Bordeaux mixture and with a mixture of 1 lb (430 g) soap and 6 lb (2.7 kg) sulphur. The last-named seemed to be the most effective treatment, but sulphur alone was quite useless. He also goes on to say that clematis may become damaged in gales with vines cracking and thus allowing fungus to enter into the broken tissues.

In his book *Garden Clematis,* published in 1959, Stanley Whitehead says that the disease has been known for over 50 years, which seems to support the idea that a hundred years ago it was unknown. He says that the fungus *Ascochyta clematindina* described by the New York Experimental Station is not the same as clematis wilt, but is a form of stem rot or leaf spot, which leaves clematis wilt unidentified with no clue as to the cause or cure.

Christopher Lloyd in his book *Clematis,* published in 1965, says,

My own unsubstantiated suspicions fall on our old enemy the grey mould fungus *Botrytis cinerea.* It is so like it to enter living plant tissue by way of a damaged or dead leaf stalk, since the large-flowering types never shed their leaves cleanly. Against this is the evidence that the fungus sometimes does its damage not at the node, but in between nodes.

My own personal pet theory, which may be quite wrong, is that it is not a disease at all but a failure of the very thin stem to cope with a sudden demand for moisture from the stem leaves and flowers. This results in a breakdown of the tissues at a certain spot. These die, causing everything above to be suddenly cut off from its life-giving sap, and consequently everything collapses. These collapses usually occur at times of high humidity when a plant is growing rapidly and requires several pints of water a day.

So my answer is to make sure your clematis have a good supply of water at the base of the roots by giving them a good soaking at least once a week. As water washes nutrients out of the soil, these must be replaced by a liberal application of a general liquid fertiliser once a week. One reason that leads me to support this theory is that clematis grown by rivers always seem to be beautiful plants, and several people who live in such spots have told me that their plants never suffer from clematis wilt. With their soil, one has only to dig down a foot or two to come upon water, which means that the plants have a constant supply of water. The stems of their plants are also much thicker than those on the plants of less fortunate people, who have to contend with hot, dry, hungry soils. Perhaps the thicker stems are more able to draw up the extra moisture demanded at peak periods without causing damage to the tissues.

One way to give the plant a constant source of water is to bury a container about 2 ft (60 cm) underneath the clematis before planting. Fill this with stones, top it up with water and cover it with peat. Then plant in the normal way. A pipe driven down to the container will enable you to top it up with water during drought periods and your clematis should have a constant supply of moisture. Even a pipe driven down to below the roots will get water down to what must be a very dry spot. Another idea I have heard of is, when a plant wilts, cut it down at once and give it a pailful of water every day for two weeks; after this shoots will appear from the roots. This is another support for the lack of moisture theory.

Another way to help to avoid clematis wilt is to layer two or three shoots around the plant, which provide the plant with extra roots. The only snag about this idea is that one has first to grow the plant to a suitable size before it can be layered, and then it takes a year for the layer to root, and it is usually during this period that wilt occurs! Once a plant has developed a good thick stem, or, as with a 'Jackmanii' variety, has several stems coming out of the ground, then wilt seldom happens.

We often get letters from customers on the subject of wilt, and Mr Jim Hodgkinson of Frodsham, near Warrington, suggests that it is caused by a symbiotic union getting out of hand, but he writes:

> I've been looking into the reason why I seem to be so lucky in not getting wilt on my clematis, whilst others seem to get 'it' so frequently, either I do something or don't do something, which others miss. One thing I have noticed is that, as you know, when the stem swells in the autumn, the epidermis splits longitudinally to reveal the tender cortex and inner portions. At this time I always spray with a fungicide (Benlate or Karathene) as, until the tissue hardens, the stem is open to attack. It could just be possible that spores enter the plant at this time and only reproduce in the spring, so that by the spring and early summer we already have fungi within the plant, which have entered, not at the height of the growing season, but in the autumn.

'Madame Julia Correvon'. A good summer-flowering variety.

Mr R. W. Sidwell of Ashton-under-Hill, near Evesham, writes:

Wilting of leaves is due to failure to replace transpirational water losses. This may be due to infection with plant pathogens and there seems no doubt that under some conditions this can be the cause of clematis wilt. Cases are, however, known where it seems improbable that infection is the primary cause.

Most plants are capable of developing a certain amount of root pressure which may be sufficient to force water to the tops of shoots but under conditions of high transpiration this is usually insufficient to replace lost water and the water columns then become in a state of tension rather than compression. This is certainly the case with clematis when at maximum water demand.

Water travels up plant stems mainly through the wood vessels which are literally water pipes. In the case of clematis these wood vessels are few in number and very large in size. They remain functional for about one year only and are replaced annually by fresh cambium growth. This exceptionally large size of wood vessel makes the water transport system of clematis particularly vulnerable. Stems with large numbers of small vessels are much better able to cope with heavy stresses in water demand.

All the cases of wilting that I have observed on planted-out plants could be explained by water shortage in the root zone, either through competition from other plants or other reasons. Plants grown in deep rich moist soil free from immediate competition have never wilted in my experience.

Wilting that I have observed is often just at peak growth, reached in early summer. This might possibly be connected with the ageing of the wood vessels before the newly developed ones are able to take over. This is pure theory but is worth investigating.

Mr Sidwell seems to support my theory, especially when he notes that plants grown in moist soil have never wilted, just as I have noticed that plants grown near rivers never wilt. So the answer here is lashings of water if your soil is light and dry.

In his slim booklet, written in 1912, William Robinson says,

What causes the clematis loss is the question all over Europe both in nurseries and in private gardens. I was led to think it was grafting that was the main reason, and, secondly, over exposure to the sun, and again the fragility of the stems, which the slightest want of care may injure, even the amount of the wind will sometimes do it. All the large kinds are grafted but if we look at the simpler kinds we find they suffer far less, and they are raised in natural ways i.e. by division, layers or seeds – in these we rarely see any signs of disease, but, on the contrary, great vigour. Even if a kind will take well on a stock when we graft a Japanese species on a European strong king (*C. vitalba*) there may be a difference in the season of a flow of sap, which may cause death. Grafting on *C. viticella* is safer, and on this stock the plants often root after being grafted. But there is no need for grafting in any case, because the plants can easily be propagated by layers and seeds, the first way being the best – the remedy for grafting is to go back to layers for all choicer kinds and it is far the best way. A veteran French nurseryman M. Jamin, told me he never regretted anything more than giving up his layering ground, that plan was adopted, no doubt, for the sake of the too facile grafting on cheap stocks that came in the way.

Layering may have been all very well in 1912 when labour was cheap and land was available but it would hardly work today and, in any case, there is no record that layers were immune from wilt. Grafting has almost vanished and is only used to produce new varieties quickly, as a grafted plant will provide cuttings three months after it is grafted. Cuttings are the main source of clematis plants nowadays, and William Robinson does not even mention them and still we have clematis wilt!

My answer to clematis wilt then is plant deeply with 3 or 4 in

'Miss Bateman'. When it first opens it has a green bar down the centre of each sepal. A good early-flowering variety.

(7.5–10 cm) of the stem below the soil, spray the base of the plant with Benlate in the autumn, again in the spring and during the summer at regular intervals. Keep the plants well watered and fed, especially during humid and quick-growing spells, make sure the soil is moist below the roots, and, with a bit of luck, this should prevent any attacks of so-called wilt.

# THE INTERNATIONAL CLEMATIS SOCIETY

he International Clematis Society was founded by Raymond Evison in 1984 with his wife Hildegard Widman-Evison acting as secretary. He was at that time Managing Director of Treasures of Tenbury Ltd, Tenbury Wells, Worcestershire. Since then he has branched out on his own in the Channel Islands and the address of the Society is now:

The International Clematis Society,
3 La Route du Coudre,
Rocquaine,
St Pierre du Bois,
Guernsey,
Channel Islands,
Great Britain

In his first Newsletter Raymond noticed that it was quite a coincidence that a hundred years previously, in 1884, one of the first books written about clematis was published in France and was written by A. Lavelle. The book was called *Les Clematites à grandes fleurs*. He also noted that is seemed quite extraordinary that, with the great surge by hybridising then taking place, a clematis society, in some form, had not been founded. Perhaps, he suggested, the advent of clematis wilt around that time dampened the enthusiasm of clematis devotees.

We are still plagued with this unfortunate malady, but with the arrival of new fungicides, and instructions to plant deep, so that there are buds below the soil which will shoot up should the notorious wilt strike, we do now stand a better chance of being successful with these lovely climbers. Also, with more realization of the plants' needs for regular feeding and watering, etc., we are in greater control than we were in the early part of the twentieth century when clematis became very unpopular. Fortunately we now have a Clematis Society which will constantly monitor new methods of dealing with clematis wilt, as well as acting as a linking medium for clematis lovers the world over. The society publishes a twice-yearly *Newsletter* full of interesting articles written by members, lists of varieties from many countries and much useful information on the genus *Clematis*.

In the first *Newsletter* Magnus Johnson of Sweden contributed an article on clematis in Sweden. Raymond described him as 'the Clematis Grandfather' to many fine hybrids and one of the most knowledgeable members of the society. Magnus Johnson said that in his country there were no nurseries growing clematis before the Second World War and that the only plants available were imported from other countries. Many plants died and it was thought that clematis were not hardy enough to survive the very low temperatures of the Swedish winters. It has since been proved, however, that most large-flowering hybrids will thrive during normal winters. In 1947 Magnus Johnson began to propagate large-flowering clematis from cuttings taken from plants that had acclimatised themselves to Swedish conditions. He also sowed seed of several varieties and selected the best types, which were tested before propagation and distribution. In his article he listed a large number of species originated in Sweden or introduced to Europe by Swedish botanists, and also listed a number of large-flowering hybrids from that country. I had the great pleasure of meeting him on two occasions when he visited England. He called at my nursery and we spent most of a lovely summer's day sitting in the walled garden, surrounded by clematis, and talking about clematis. He is a delightful person and I greatly enjoyed the privilege of meeting him.

Richard Pennell, another well-known name in the clematis world, also wrote an article in this first *Newsletter*. This was about the work of his father Walter Pennell, especially during the years 1950–62. It was during this time that Walter Pennell concentrated on hybridising clematis and produced such famous varieties as 'Bracebridge Star', 'H. F. Young', 'John Warren', 'Kathleen Wheeler', 'Lincoln Star', 'Mrs N. Thompson' and 'Vyvyan Pennell'. This last one is the most famous of all – a wonderful fully double variety with purple, violet and crimson colours, the most popular double of all. Since then two new varieties have arrived, 'Walter Pennell' and 'Richard Pennell', father and son, both of which are becoming very popular. In all 26 new varieties were produced in that period, most of them with detailed information of the varieties from which the crosses were made, the date sown, the date first flowered and the descriptions. If only we kept records like that!

Mrs Harvey of Kitchener, Ontario, Canada also contributed an interesting article. She started off 'I do not operate a nursery' but apparently she has been growing hybrids and species in her garden for many years and distributing them all over the world. She says she has at least 80 species in her small garden but she has managed to persuade the director of the Royal Botanical Gardens at Hamilton to set aside an area to be specially devoted to clematis and she has generously given many of her plants to this garden. It is known as 'Mrs Harvey's Clematis Garden' and is well worth a visit if you are ever in Ontario.

In a later edition of the *Newsletter* Raymond tells how he visited Kitchener during his lecture tour of America and arrived in time for the opening of this clematis garden. He said that Mrs Harvey is a delightful person and was in fine form that afternoon.

Mrs Harvey's article finished by saying that she wished that clematis were better known and that botanical gardens and arboretums would grow them to a greater extent and that perhaps the International Clematis Society would encourage the use of this beautiful genus.

In 1977 the Director of Regents Park in London wrote to me saying that he was going to build a pergola in the park devoted entirely to clematis. We took a load of plants there when we were on our way to Bournemouth for a holiday.

Another spot in London where clematis can be seen is the attractive garden in Eccleston Square. This is a private garden belonging to the residents of the square, who have renovated the garden, planting new shrubs and plants, etc. Round the outside railings they have planted clematis so that the public will also be able to enjoy them. We supplied the plants together with Raymond Evison, and as we stay at the Eccleston Hotel when at the Chelsea Flower Show, we can keep an eye on them.

Arthur Steffen of Steffen's Clematis Nursery at Fairport, New York, USA also had a small article in this first *Newsletter*, telling how his world-famous nursery began growing clematis in 1950. Previously they had been growing geraniums and were looking round for a plant which had less competition. They hit on clematis and now they grow over a million plants a year and have 25 greenhouses covering 90,000 sq ft (8,361 sq m).

The Society continued to expand and by the time the second *Newsletter* appeared the membership had risen to 250 with twenty countries represented. Raymond contributed an interesting account of his tour of Japan, China and Poland, finding several varieties of clematis species growing wild. At the Great Wall of China he found plants of *C. brevicaudata, C. aethusifolia* and *C. hexapetala,* on the slopes of Mount Fuji a creeping form of *C. alpina ochotensis,* and in a valley near Nikko the white form of *C. patens.* In Poland he met Brother Stefan Franczak, who has introduced several very good varieties, such as 'Jan Pawel II' (John Paul II), 'Kardynal Wyszynski', 'Kacper' and 'Warszawska Nike' (pronounced neekay).

Rex Wild of Murrambee, Victoria, Australia related his experiences in growing clematis 'Down Under' for 40 years. Importing clematis into Australia is very difficult and plants have to be kept in quarantine for one year. Rex lost so many plants this way that he obtained permission to have a small quarantine area on his own property. With this method the survival rate was greatly improved, but the facility was later withdrawn, and the survival rate went down once more. Clematis have to be sent bare-rooted, from the winter of Britain to the summer of Australia, so it is no wonder that success

'Mrs Spencer Castle'. An unusual colour, with double flowers in June and July and single flowers on the young wood in September.

was limited. Rex Wild complained that in his country many varieties were incorrectly labelled, but I fear that Australia is not the only country where this happens!

Where Rex lives in Victoria there is a village called Clematis! It was originally named Paradise, so it was no wonder that the inhabitants changed the name in 1921. The reason for choosing Clematis was because of the wild Australian clematis *C. aristata*, an evergreen with small white flowers, which grows in profusion along the fences in that locality. Clematis is in an area of hills, lakes and forests known as the Dandenong Ranges and, as it is only 20 miles (32 km) from Melbourne, it is the natural playground of that city. When Rex first told me about this I asked him to send me a letter from there with the Clematis postmark to put in our catalogue, but he wrote back to say that the post office had been closed down and transferred to Emerald, a nearby town. This was a great pity, but anyway he sent me a Clematis T-shirt which I threatened to wear at the Chelsea Flower Show until the rest of the staff objected! I did offer to buy them one each but they thought it would let the side down and lower the tone of the show!

The first conference of the Clematis Society was held at the Royal

Horticultural Society's headquarters in London in 1985, and although only 50 members attended, it was a great success. The conference lasted five days and several members gave talks. In the hall where one of the RHS fortnightly shows was being held, there was a magnificent display of paintings of clematis and photographs and papers contributed by members. For this exhibition the society was awarded the RHS Lindley Silver Medal. This medal is given for an exhibition of scientific and educational value, and was a source of great delight to members. Magnus Johnson was awarded the RHS Grenfell Silver Gilt medal for his exhibition of clematis paintings, which he and his family brought over from Sweden, and which were greatly admired.

One of the talks at the conference was by Frieda Brown, whose garden in Leeds is becoming quite famous. It has appeared on television several times and has been featured in garden magazines. Nothing remarkable about that you may think, but Frieda's garden is at the back of a council house at Moor Green Estate in Leeds and is a long narrow strip, 120 ft (36 m) long by 25 ft (8 m) wide! With her husband Joe she has created a marvellous garden; there are two ponds, archways, a patio, a herbaceous border, grass and camomile lawns, a fern garden and an alpine setting, all enclosed by fences covered with various climbers. The great speciality of the garden, however, is clematis. Sixty varieties cover the archways and fences.

At the conference Frieda described her 'small is beautiful' garden and she concluded by saying,

> We open the garden in the summer for various charities and many of the visitors come especially to see the clematis collection. My joy is to talk and encourage them to grow more clematis; many are hesitant and the overall impression I get from talking to them is that they think that clematis are difficult to cultivate. Of course when they look around our very small garden and see the effect of 60 varieties all growing happily, and then look at the gardener responsible, they say to themselves, 'Well, if she can do this so can I'.

One of the aims of the society is to help Dr Brandenburg, the registrar for clematis, with his work in preparing the clematis register.

He appealed to members to help him, saying that he already had a checklist of 900 cultivars, which seems to be an incredible number. These must be double checked of course, which is quite a job, but he is being assisted by J. G. van de Vooren at the Agriculture University in the Netherlands. They asked members wishing to register any cultivars of recent introduction to fill in a form, which was printed in two *Newsletters*, and return it to Dr Brandenburg. This form requested details of the parents, or chance seedling, year first bloomed and description of the cultivars in detail. These data are being processed by computer and by this method arrangements of the cultivar – its name and group or country of origin – can easily be made. Dr Brandenburg and J. G. van de Vooren hope to supplement the clematis register

'Mrs N. Thompson'.
A striking contrast in
colour and very free-
flowering.

with a collection of illustrations and specimens, which is sometimes the only possible way to determine the identity of certain clematis cultivars.

In one of the *Newsletters* there was a list of well over a hundred varieties raised in the Soviet Union since 1958. Most of these seem to be crosses between varieties available in Western Europe and America but all the names are quite different from any of our clematis and, as far as I know, none of them is available in Britain. Neither is there any mention of the possibility of any being exported, which is a great pity as I am sure there must be a number of excellent clematis amongst such descriptions as 'amethyst violet', 'spectrum violet', 'light phlox purple', 'light orchid violet', 'amaranth rose', 'Bishop's purple', etc.

Japan, on the other hand, is keen to get its varieties over to the

Western world and in an article entitled 'My Clematis Collection' Mr Kaneshige says he wishes to advise us that some of the Japanese varieties are very beautiful. He wonders why more European people do not cultivate them and hopes that European nurserymen will include them in their catalogues. We have sent a large number of clematis to Mr Kaneshige over the years, and have already taken note of his complaint and imported several varieties from his country, which will appear in our catalogue from time to time.

In another article Mr Kaneshige describes how the Japanese grow many varieties in tubs and large containers, which produce up to two hundred flowers. His advice is to give them plenty of water every day and liquid fertiliser three times a week! I should have thought that this was excessive but if it produces these spectacular results then it is worth trying, although very time-consuming.

Kaneshige says he has 150 large-flowering varieties in containers and over 60 of the species, so this should encourage us to grow them in this way in Britain.

If you cannot grow clematis planted in a garden then this is an ideal alternative. You can stand the containers on a terrace or patio when the clematis are in flower, moving them to another place in the garden for the winter. They can then be left out of the way until they flower. For support you can use canes, trellis and Netlon.

I well remember seeing a magnificent display of clematis at a Chelsea Flower Show in the 1940s. This was by Bees of Chester and they had a large square filled with tubs and containers of clematis, some on the ground and those in the centre on pedestals. Each variety was a mass of bloom and the whole effect was a sea of clematis flowers. They were awarded a well deserved Gold Medal but I cannot recall ever seeing them there again, but it proves that we knew about growing clematis in containers even then. In fact, in the 1877 Jackman and Moore book on clematis there is a whole chapter devoted to the art of growing them in tubs.

Some of the articles in the *Newsletters* are naturally on the learned side, with long lists of varieties described in detail, so I was pleased to see a humorous article appearing. Vic Howe of Brighton introduced some of this much-needed light relief in an article in which he said he wouldn't know an F1 from an F2 if it came up and hit him on the nose and that his technical knowledge of gardening, after three years, would still be hard pressed to cover a pinhead. Slugs and snails were ruining his clematis by using them as their invalid diet. They shared this passion with herds of woodlice that rampaged around the garden. He said,

I have heard that cinders are a very good repellent, but as I do not have an open fire I decided to use slug pellets. They were a complete waste of time and within a week all my plants have been attacked. Poor Betty Balfour had been completely stripped, I really thought I had lost her. Explaining that I had her best

'Nelly Moser'. The well-known variety will fade badly in full sun, so plant it on a north-facing wall or in shade.

interests at heart I told her that I would have to resort to unorthodox tactics to try and save her. My first line of attack was emptying my ashtrays at the base of the plants; raking the soil over lightly stopped them making an unsightly mess. I can't claim any outstanding success but it does seem to put some pests off and I'm hoping that the rest will take up the habit and smoke themselves to an early demise. Another tactic I tried is planting garlic alongside my clematis. I am now looking for a French hedgehog who would like to take up residence and eat my garlic flavoured slugs and snails. The garlic certainly seems to have protected all plants except Betty Balfour whom I have found twice completely naked. I am beginning to suspect that she is not as good as she might be, and maybe ought to change her name to Mae West!

The article was accompanied by cartoon drawings of poor 'Betty Balfour' being attacked by cigarette-smoking woodlice.

An excellent article was entitled 'Clematis – an amateur's experi-ence', by John G. Howells, in which he remarked that the *Newsletter* was full of interest, but largely for the professional grower, with which I agree, and so it was interesting to read his comments. He lists his favourite clematis, which are mainly of the early-flowering hybrids. I was rather surprised to see that he did not include any of the lovely long-flowering 'Jackmanii' varieties, especially my own favourite 'Perle d'Azur'. His guidance on planting is excellent and well worth including in this book. He says he has found a foolproof way of planting clematis! I wish he had told us about this years ago! On our hungry soil on the east coast of Suffolk we suffer disappointments unless we feed and water often, so his technique is of great interest to those who fail to grow clematis successfully. First of all he says we must start with a good plant. Then dig the usual 18 in (45 cm) square hole, well away from the wall or tree on which the plant is to climb. In the bottom put half the contents of a good tomato growbag. Improve this with a handful of 6X (chicken manure) for immediate stimulation and a handful of bonemeal for long-term effect. A little more of the peat is put on top of this to prevent the roots coming into contact with the strong bottom peat too soon. The rest of the growbag goes into the top half and in this is planted the clematis. A good watering and one seems to get a good result every time! It is rather an expensive method if one is planting several clematis, but for the odd one or two it should be well worth the cost.

His feeding method is as follows. In March give each plant a handful of 6X and a handful of potash. Repeat this in July for later-flowering varieties. He is a busy man, he says, but if he has time he gives them a liquid feed during the summer and suggests that Tomorite is excellent for this purpose. He says that wilt is not a problem with him although a 'William Kennett' did wilt three times before making a good plant. He sprays his plants with a combined fungicide and pesticide in the spring and repeats this three weeks later, with another spray in midsummer if he has time!

This is what the Clematis Society is all about, sharing problems and successes with fellow members and all lovers of clematis. Perhaps if Dr Howells had come up with his suggestions many years ago there would not have been so many people who have given up growing clematis in despair. Let's hope they will try again and that we shall see everyone making the most of clematis, and succeeding.

Dr Howells is now the Editor of the Clematis Societies *Journal* which has replaced the Newsletter and one of his first jobs was to find out the ten most popular clematis. A questionnaire was sent to volunteer members from ten countries and the result was:

Most popular variety – 'Perle d'Azur'
Second – *C. viticella* varieties
Third – 'Marie Boisellot'
Fourth – *C. orientalis*
Fifth – 'Jackmanii'
Sixth – *Lasurstern*
Seventh – *C. montana* varieties
Eighth – 'Dr Ruppel'
Ninth – *C. alpina* and *C. macropetela* varieties
Tenth – 'The President' and *C. texensis* varieties.

I was pleased to see that my favourite clematis had topped the Poll, also that one of our introductions, Dr Ruppel, was included in the top ten, the only new variety since the Second World War to be included, all the others having been popular for up to one hundred years or more.

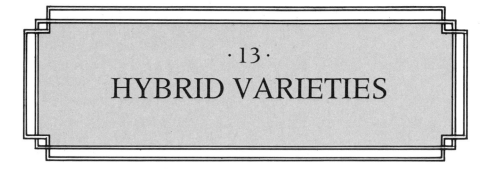

# · 13 ·
# HYBRID VARIETIES

hese large-flowering hybrids are given in alphabetical order, stating the main characteristics of each variety: the colour and size of bloom; the approximate height to which they grow, although this and the size of flower will vary from place to place; their flowering period; which group they belong to; how they should be pruned.

Clematis are divided into groups, bringing together those varieties that are similar in habit and character, thus giving us their times of flowering and their needs for pruning. Clematis used to be catalogued under each group, which made things rather confusing, but nowadays they are listed in alphabetical order in most catalogues, often with a letter beside each variety indicating the group to which that variety belongs. With the introduction of many new varieties I feel that the groups are now so intermixed that any reference to them in catalogues is both unhelpful and confusing to the vast majority of gardeners.

As the groups have become so intermingled during the last hundred years of cross-breeding, it is not always clear to which group certain varieties belong. The main trouble is with the *patens* and *lanuginosa* varieties which have become so mixed that it is difficult to separate them. However, I have attempted to do this by listing under the *patens* group all those that flower on year-old ripened wood in May and June and do not flower again until September, when they do so with smaller flowers on the young wood produced during the summer. In the *lanuginosa* group I have listed all those varieties that flower on year-old ripened wood in May and June and throughout the summer at intervals on young wood produced in the early summer. The 'Jackmanii' and *viticella* groups are those that flower on the young wood from June to the end of October and they are the ones that really do need hard pruning every winter.

'No pruning' in the description means *do not prune* under any circumstances during the winter or early spring, otherwise you will lose the spectacular flowers of May and June. They can be trimmed in February, cutting the dead ends of the stems back to live buds, but that is all that is necessary.

'Prune hard' means that these varieties should be cut down as low as possible during the winter or early spring, as they flower during the summer and autumn on the young wood only, which is produced during the spring and early summer.

'Pruning optional' means that these varieties bloom equally well on both young and old wood and can be left unpruned if an early show of flowers is desired, or pruned during the winter or early spring if a summer show is required.

Details of origins of varieties have been left out, as with most of them there are no records of where they were raised or the raiser, and this is of little interest to the general gardener who merely wants to know what colour the plant is, how high it will grow, and how it should be pruned. For this reason I have also left out the technical details of leaf formation, number of sepals to each bloom, etc. The size of flowers and height of plants are only approximate as they will vary from place to place.

The description is given first, followed by time of flowering, approximate size of flower, approximate height of plant, group and, finally, pruning.

## Large-flowering hybrids

'Alice Fisk'   Wisteria-blue with long pointed sepals, crenulated edges and dark brown stamens. Flowering May, June and again in September. Size of flowers, 6–8 in (15–20 cm). Grows to an approximate height of 6–8 ft (2–2.5 m). *Patens* group. No pruning necessary.

'Allanah'   Bright ruby-red with spaced sepals, dark brown stamens. June to September. Flowers 6–8 in (15–20 cm). Height 6–8 ft (2–2.5 m). *Jackmanii* group. Prune hard.

'Annabel'   Good mid-blue with a white centre. A large stiff bloom. Flowering May and June. Flowers 6–8 in (15–20 cm). Height 6–8 ft (2–2.5 m). *Patens* group. No pruning.

'Appare'   Blue-violet with rose-purple stamens. Flowering May and June. Flowers 7–9 in (17–22 cm). Height 6–8 ft (2–2.5 m). *Patens* group. No pruning.

'Asao'   Reddish-pink with a white bar, brown stamens. June to September. Flowers 6–8 in (15–20 cm). Height 6–8 ft (2–2.5 m). *Jackmanii* group. Prune hard.

'Ascotiensis'   Bright blue with pointed sepals, green stamens. July to September continuously. Flowers 6–8 in (15–20 cm). Height 8–12 ft. (2.5–3.5 m). *Jackmanii* group. Prune hard.

'Niobe'. A lovely deep colour, almost black when first opening.

*C. orientalis*. A close-up of this splendid species. In the autumn it is covered with attractive seedheads.

'Barbara Dibley'    Petunia-red flowers with deep carmine bars on each sepal, long tapering sepals and dark stamens. May and June. Flowers 6–8 in (15–20 cm). Height 6–8 ft (2–2.5 m). *Patens* group. No pruning.

'Barbara Jackman'    Petunia-mauve with crimson bars and cream stamens. May and June. Flowers 5–7 in (13–17 cm). Height 6–8 ft (2–2.5 m). *Patens* group. No pruning.

'Beauty of Richmond'    Pale lavender-blue with a light chocolate centre. June to August. Flowers 6–8 in (15–20 cm). Height 8–12 ft (2.5–3.5 m). *Lanuginosa* group. Pruning optional.

'Beauty of Worcester'    Deep double blue with white stamens in May and June. Single flowers from June to September. Flowers 5–7 in (13–17 cm). Height 6–8 ft (2–2.5 m). *Florida* group. No pruning.

'Bees Jubilee'    Mauve-pink with deep carmine bars, brown stamens. May, June and again in September. Flowers 6–8 in (15–20 cm). Height 6–8 ft. (2–2.5 m). *Patens* group. No pruning.

'Belle Nantaise'    Lavender-blue with long pointed sepals and white stamens. June to September. Flowers 8–10 in (20–25 cm). Height 6–8 ft (2–2.5 m). *Lanuginosa* group. Pruning optional.

'Belle of Woking'    Double silvery-mauve, rosette-shaped flowers, yellow stamens. May and June. Flowers 6–8 in (15–20 cm). Height 6–8 ft (2–2.5 m). *Florida* group. No pruning.

'Blue Diamond'    Sky-blue with overlapping sepals and white stamens. May and June. Flowers 6–8 in (15–20 cm). Height 8–12 ft (2.5–3.5 m). *Patens* group. No pruning.

'Blue Gem'    Pale lavender-blue with dark stamens. May to September. Flowers 6–8 in (15–20 cm). Height 8–12 ft (2.5–3.5 m). *Lanuginosa* group. Pruning optional.

'Bracebridge Star'    Lavender-blue with carmine bar and dark stamens. May to September. Flowers 6–8 in (15–20 cm). Height 8–12 ft (2.5–3.5 m). *Lanuginosa* group. Pruning optional.

'Capitan Thuilleaux'    Broad strawberry-pink bars on cream background, pointed sepals and golden brown stamens. May and June. Flowers 6–8 in (15–20 cm). Height 6–8 ft (2–2.5 m). *Patens* group. No pruning.

*C. paniculata.*
Originally called *C.*
*indivisa lobata*. A
native of New
Zealand, it requires a
warm corner.

'Carnaby'    Deep raspberry-pink with a deeper bar and golden
brown stamens. May and June. Flowers 6–8 in (15–20 cm). Height
6–8 ft (2–2.5 m). *Patens* group. No pruning.

'Chalcedony'    Ice-blue double in both early and late summer.
May, June and September. Flowers 4–6 in (10–15 cm). Height
6–8 ft (2–2.5 m). *Patens* group. No pruning.

'Charissima'    Cerise-pink with maroon centre and deeper bar with delicate veining. May and June. Flowers 6–8 in (15–20 cm). Height 8–12 ft (2.5–3.5 m). *Patens* group. No pruning.

'Comtesse de Bouchaud'    Mauve-pink with cream stamens. Very free-flowering; June to September continuously. Flowers 4–6 in (10–15 cm). Height 6–8 ft (2–2.5 m). *Jackmanii* group. Prune hard.

'Corona'    Deep purple with pink shading, dark red stamens. May, June and September. Flowers 6–8 in (15–20 cm). Height 6–8 ft (2–2.5 m). *Patens* group. No pruning.

'Countess of Lovelace'    Double bluish-lilac, rosette-shaped flowers, single on young wood. June to September. Flowers 6–8 in (15–20 cm). Height 6–8 ft (2–2.5 m). *Florida* group. No pruning.

'Crimson King'    Crimson-red with brown stamens. June to September. Flowers 6–8 in (15–20 cm). Height 8–12 ft (2.5–3.5 m). *Lanuginosa* group. Pruning optional.

'C. W. Dowman'    Lavender-pink with deep bar and golden stamens. June to September. Flowers 4–6 in (10–15 cm). Height 6–8 ft (2–2.5 m). *Lanuginosa* group. Pruning optional.

'Daniel Deronda'    Semi-double violet-blue with creamy stamens. May and June. Single flowers from June to September. Flowers 6–8 in (15–20 cm). Height 6–8 ft (2–2.5 m). *Florida* group. No pruning.

'Dawn'    Pearly-pink with overlapping sepals and carmine stamens – a good compact plant. May and June. Flowers 6–8 in (15–20 cm). Height 6–8 ft (2–2.5 m). *Patens* group. No pruning.

'Dr Ruppel'    Rose madder with a brilliant carmine bar and golden stamens. May and June. Flowers 6–8 in (15–20 cm). Height 6–8 ft (2–2.5 m). *Patens* group. No pruning.

'Duchess of Edinburgh'    Double white rosette-shaped blooms from June to September. Flowers 4–6 in (10–15 cm). Height 6–8 ft (2–2.5 m). *Florida* group. No pruning.

'Duchess of Sutherland'    Mottled wine-red with lighter bar and golden stamens. June to September. Flowers 5–7 in (13–17 cm). Height 6–8 ft (2–2.5 m). *Lanuginosa* group. Pruning optional.

'Prince Charles' flowers all summer long. A good clematis for small gardens, it comes from New Zealand.

116

'Edouard Desfosse'    Deep mauve-purple with deeper bar and reddish-purple stamens. May and June. Flowers 7−9 in (17−22 cm). Height 6−8 ft (2−2.5 m). *Patens* group. No pruning.

'Edith'    Clear white with dark red stamens. A seedling from 'Mrs Cholmondeley' retaining this variety's character. June to September. Flowers 6−8 in (15−20 cm). Height 6−8 ft (2−2.5m). *Lanuginosa* group. Pruning optional.

'Elizabeth Foster'    Delicate pink with deep carmine bars, maroon centre. Firm saucer-shaped flowers. May and June. Flowers 6−8 in (15−20 cm). Height 6−8 ft (2−2.5 m). *Patens* group. No pruning.

'Elsa Spath' see 'Xerxes'.

'Ernest Markham'    Glowing petunia-red with blunt-tipped sepals and golden stamens. July to October continuously. Flowers 4−6 in (10−15 cm). Height 8−12 ft (2.5−3.5 m). *Viticella* group. Prune hard.

'Etoile de Paris'    Mauve-blue with pointed sepals and red anthers. May and June. Flowers 6−8 in (15−20 cm). Height 6−8 ft (2−2.5 m). *Patens* group. No pruning.

'Etoile Violette'    Deep purple, with blunt-tipped sepals and golden stamens. Very free and vigorous. July to September continuously. Flowers 4−5 in (10−13 cm). Height 12−20 ft (3.5−6 m). *Viticella* group. Prune hard.

'Ewa'    White with a touch of pink, and dark stamens. Flowers June to September. Flowers 6−8 in (15−20 cm). Height 6−8 ft (2−2.5 m). *Lanuginosa* group. Pruning optional.

'Fair Rosamond'    Blush-white with red bars and purple stamens; has a slight scent of violets. June to September. Flowers 4−6 in (10−15 cm). Height 6−8 ft (2−2.5 m). *Lanuginosa* group. Pruning optional.

'Fairy Queen'    Flesh-coloured with rosy bars and dark anthers. May and June. Flowers 6−8 in (15−20 cm). Height 6−8 ft (2−2.5 m). *Patens* group. No pruning.

'Four Star'    Pale lavender with a deeper bar. May, June and September. Flowers 6−8 in (15−20 cm). Height 6−8 ft (2−2.5 m). *Patens* group. No pruning.

'General Sikorski'    Mid-blue with crenulated edges and golden stamens. June to September. Flowers 6−8 in (15−20 cm). Height 6−8 ft (2−2.5 m). *Lanuginosa* group. Pruning optional.

'Prins Hendrik' is grown in greenhouses in Holland as a cut flower. It is difficult in the garden in Britain, but fine in Australia where this photograph was taken.

'Gillian Blades'     Pure white with long flat sepals with frilled edges and golden stamens. May and June. Flowers 7−9 in (17−22 cm). Height 6−8 ft (2−2.5 m). *Patens* group. No pruning.

'Gipsy Queen'     Rich violet-purple with a velvet sheen, reddish-purple stamens. Very free and vigorous. July to October continuously. Flowers 4−6 in (10−15 cm). Height 8−12 ft (2.5−3.5 m). *Viticella* group. Prune hard.

'Gladys Picard'     Delicate mauve-pink with deeper pink bar, overlapping pointed sepals and golden stamens. May and June. Flowers 6−8 in (15−20 cm). Height 6−8 ft (2−2.5 m). *Patens* group. No pruning.

'Guiding Star'     Light purple with dark stamens. June to September. Flowers 6−8 in (15−20 cm). Height 6−8 ft (2−2.5 m). *Jackmanii* group. Prune hard.

'Hagley Hybrid'     Shell-pink with cup-shaped pointed sepals and brown stamens. Very free-flowering, June to September continuously. Flowers 4−6 in (10−15 cm). Height 6−8 ft (2−2.5 m). *Jackmanii* group. Prune hard.

'Halina Noll'   Double white large flat flower tinged with pink. May and June. Single flowers from June to September. Flowers 8–10 in (20–25 cm). Height 8–12 ft (2.5–3.5 m). *Florida* group. No pruning.

'Haku Ookan'   Lustrous violet with striking white stamens. Semi-double in May and June. Single from June to September. Flowers 6–8 in (15–20 cm). Height 6–8 ft (2–2.5 m). *Florida* group. No pruning.

'Helen Cropper'   Deep rosy-pink with red stamens. A magnificent flower. May, June and September. Flowers 6–8 in (15–20 cm). Height 6–8 ft (2–2.5 m). *Patens* group. No pruning.

'Henryi'   Creamy-white with dark stamens and handsome pointed sepals. Makes a good cut flower. June to September. Flowers 6–8 in (15–20 cm). Height 8–12 ft (2.5–3.5 m). *Lanuginosa* group. Pruning optional.

'Herbert Johnson'   Reddish-mauve with maroon centre. Very free-flowering variety. June to September. Flowers 6–8 in (15–20 cm). Height 6–8 ft (2–2.5 m). *Patens* group. No pruning.

'H. F. Young'   Wedgwood-blue pointed overlapping sepals with cream stamens. Very free-flowering. May and June. Flowers 6–8 in (15–20 cm). Height 8–12 ft (2.5–3.5 m). *Patens* group. No pruning.

'Hidcote Purple'   Royal purple suffused with claret. June to September. Flowers 4–6 in (10–15 cm). Height 6–8 ft (2–2.5 m). *Lanuginosa* group. Pruning optional.

'Horn of Plenty'   Rosy-purple with a deeper bar, reddish purple stamens. June to September. Flowers 6–8 in (15–20 cm). Height 8–12 ft (2.5–3.5 m). *Lanuginosa* group. Pruning optional.

'Huldine'   Pearly-white with pale mauve bars on the reverse of the sepals. Very vigorous and free-flowering. June to October continuously. Flowers 2–4 in (5–10 cm). Height 12–20 ft (3.5–6 m). *Viticella* group. Prune hard.

'Jackmanii'   Dark velvety-purple four-sepalled flowers with green stamens. Masses of flowers throughout the summer. The most popular clematis yet raised. June to September continuously. Flowers 4–6 in (10–15 cm). Height 10–20 ft (3–6 m). *Jackmanii* group. Prune hard.

'Jackmanii Alba'   The white variety of 'Jackmanii' which sometimes produces double bluish ragged flowers early in the season. Very

*C. recta* makes a good herbaceous plant. It is sweetly scented.

strong and free-flowering. June to September. Flowers 4–6 in (10–15 cm). Height 10–20 ft (3–6 m). *Jackmanii* group. Prune hard.

'Jackmanii Rubra'    The red 'Jackmanii'; petunia-red with cream stamens. Just as free-flowering as its parent. Will sometimes produce double flowers early in the season. June to September continuously. Flowers 4–6 in (10–15 cm). Height 10–20 ft (3–6 m). *Jackmanii* group. Prune hard.

'Jackmanii Superba'    Similar to 'Jackmanii' but with broader sepals which makes it a fuller flower. June to September continuously. Flowers 4–6 in (10–15 cm). Height 10–20 ft (3–6 m). *Jackmanii* group. Prune hard.

'James Mason'    White with crimped sepals and maroon stamens. May, June and September. Flowers 6–8 in (15–20 cm). Height 6–8 ft (2–2.5 m). *Patens* group. No pruning.

'Jan Pawel II' (John Paul II)    Creamy white with pink shading which becomes a distinct bar in late summer. Brown stamens. May, June and September. Flowers 6–8 in (15–20 cm). Height 6–8 ft (2–2.5 m). *Patens* group. No pruning.

'Joan Picton'     Glowing wild lilac with brown stamens. Very free-flowering. June to September. Flowers 6–8 in (15–20 cm). Height 6–8 ft (2–2.5 m). *Patens* group. No pruning.

'Joan Wilcox'     Soft lilac with a deeper bar, crenulated edges with golden stamens. May and June. Flowers 7–9 in (17–22 cm). Height 8–12 ft (2.5–3.5 m). *Patens* group. No pruning.

'John Warren'     Carmine edging on a French grey base with carmine bars, overlapping pointed sepals and brown stamens. June to September. Flowers 6–8 in (15–20 cm). Height 6–8 ft (2–2.5 m). *Lanuginosa* group. Pruning optional.

'Kacper'     Intense violet with dark stamens. May, June and September. Flowers 6–8 in (15–20 cm). Height 6–8 ft (2–2.5 m) *Lanuginosa* group. Pruning optional.

'Kardynal Wyszynski'     Glowing crimson with brown stamens. June to September. Flowers 6–8 in (15–20 cm). Height 6–8 ft (2–2.5 m). *Jackmanii* group. Prune hard.

'Kathleen Dunford'     Rich rosy-purple, with golden stamens. Semi-double in May and June, single blooms later in summer. Flowers 7–9 in (17–22 cm). Height 6–8 ft (2–2.5 m). *Florida* group. No pruning.

'Kathleen Wheeler'     Gorgeous plummy-mauve with striking golden stamens. June and July and again in September. Flowers 8–10 in (20–25 cm). Height 6–8 ft (2–2.5 m). *Patens* group. No pruning.

'Keith Richardson'     Deep crimson-rose with a bold white centre. May, June and September. Flowers 6–8 in (15–20 cm). Height 6–8 ft (2–2.5 m). *Patens* group. No pruning.

'King Edward VII'     Puce-violet with a pale crimson bar. June to August. Flowers 6–8 in (15–20 cm). Height 6–8 ft (2–2.5 m). *Lanuginosa* group. Pruning optional.

'King George V'     Flesh-pink with bright pink bars and brown stamens. July and August. Flowers 4–6 in (10–15 cm). Height 6–8 ft (2–2.5 m). *Lanuginosa* group. Pruning optional.

'Lady Betty Balfour'     Violet-blue with yellow stamens. Vigorous

*C. rehderiana*, a vigorous grower, flowers in late summer and autumn and smells of cowslips.

and free-flowering but needs full sun, as it is late-flowering. September and October. Flowers 6−8 in (15−20 cm). Height 10−20 ft (3−6 m). *Viticella* group. Prune hard.

'Lady Caroline Nevill'    Lavender-blue with darker bar and beige stamens. Sometimes produces semi-double flowers in the season. June to October. Flowers 6−8 in (15−20 cm). Height 8−12 ft (2.5−3.5 m). *Lanuginosa* group. Pruning optional.

'Lady Londesborough'    Mauve, paling to silvery-grey with dark stamen. June to September. Flowers 6−8 in (10−15 cm). Height 6−8 ft (2−2.5 m). *Lanuginosa* group. Pruning optional.

'Lady Northcliffe'    Deep wedgwood-blue with white stamens. Compact and free-flowering. June to September. Flowers 4−6 in (10−15 cm). Height 6−8 ft (2−2.5 m). *Lanuginosa* group. Pruning optional.

'Lasurstern'    Handsome rich deep blue with wavy sepals and contrasting white stamens. May, June and September. Flowers 7−9 in (17−22 cm). Height 8−12 ft (2.5−3.5 m). *Patens* group. No pruning.

'Laura'    Bright lilac with brown stamens. July to October. Flowers 4–6 in (10–15 cm). Height 6–8 ft (2–2.5 m). *Lanuginosa* group. Pruning optional.

'Laura Denny'    Creamy white with pink stamens. Very free flowering. May, June and September. Flowers 4–6 in (10–15 cm). Height 6–8 ft (2–2.5 cm). *Patens* group. No pruning.

'Lawsoniana'    Lavender-blue with a rosy tint, long pointed sepals and pale brown stamens. Flowers 8–10 in (20–25 cm). Height 8–12 ft (2.5–3.5 m). *Lanuginosa* group. Pruning optional.

'Lilacina Floribunda'    Deep purple with dark stamens. June to September. Flowers 4–6 in (10–15 cm). Height 6–8 ft (2–2.5 m). *Lanuginosa* group. No pruning.

'Lincoln Star'    Cochineal-pink with paler edges, pointed sepals and maroon centre. May, June and September. Flowers 6–8 in (15–20 cm). Height 6–8 ft (2–2.5 m). *Patens* group. No pruning.

'Lord Nevill'    Rich deep blue with crenulated sepals and purple stamens. May, June and September. Flowers 6–8 in (15–20 cm). Height 6–8 ft (2–2.5 m). *Patens* group. No pruning.

'Louise Rowe'    Double pale mauve, single, semi-double and double flowers all at the same time. Golden stamens. May, June and September. Flowers 4–6 in (10–15 cm). Height 6–8 ft (2–2.5 m). *Florida* group. No pruning.

'Lucey'    Lavender-pink with brown stamens. June to September. Flowers 4–6 in (10–15 cm). Height 6–8 ft (2–2.5 m). *Jackmanii* group. Prune hard.

'Madame Baron Veillard'    Lilac-rose pointed sepals with white stamens. Vigorous and free-flowering. September to October continuously. Flowers 4–6 in (10–15 cm). Height 8–12 ft (2.5–3.5 m). *Jackmanii* group. Prune hard.

'Madame Edouard André'    Deep wine-red with pointed sepals and cream stamens. June to September continuously. Flowers 4–6 in (10–15 cm). Height 6–8 ft (2–2.5 m). *Jackmanii* group. Prune hard.

'Madame Grange'    Dusky purple with incurving sepals revealing a silvery reverse. Dark stamens. August to October continuously. Flowers 4–6 in (10–15 cm). Height 6–8 ft (2–2.5 m). *Jackmanii* group. Prune hard.

'Royalty'. Semi-double clematis are rare; this is one of the best.

'Madame Julia Correvon'   Deep wine-red twisted sepals with golden stamens. Very free-flowering. June to September continuously. Flowers 2−4 in (5−10 cm). Height 6−8 ft (2−2.5 m). *Viticella* group. Prune hard.

'Madame le Coultre'   See 'Marie Boisellot'. The same variety which has two names.

'Marcel Moser'   Soft petunia-mauve with deep carmine bars on the long pointed sepals. Reddish-purple stamens. May, June and September. Flowers 7−9 in (17−22 cm). Height 6−8 ft (2−2.5 m). *Patens* group. No pruning.

'Margot Koster'   Mauve-pink spaced sepals. Vigorous and free-flowering. July and August continuously. Flowers 2−4 in (5−10 cm). Height 6−8 ft (2−2.5 m). *Viticella* group. Hard pruning.

'Marie Boisellot'   Pure white with wavy overlapping sepals and pale yellow stamens. Vigorous and free-flowering. Also known as 'Madame le Coultre'. June to September. Flowers 6−8 in (15−20 cm). Height 12−16 ft (3.5−5 m). *Lanuginosa* group. Pruning optional.

125

'Margaret Hunt'    Lavender-pink flowers with brown stamens. Vigorous and free-flowering. June to September continuously. Flowers 4–6 in (10–15 cm). Height 8–12 ft (2.5–3.5 m). *Jackmanii* group. Prune hard.

'Matka Teresa' (Mother Teresa)    White with crenulated edges and dark brown stamens. July to October. Flowers 6–8 in (15–20 cm). Height 8–12 ft (2.5–3.5 m). *Lanuginosa* group. Pruning optional.

'Maureen'    Rich royal purple with a velvety sheen. June to September. Flowers 6–8 in (15–20 cm). Height 6–8 ft (2–2.5 m). *Lanuginosa* group. Pruning optional.

'Miriam Markham'    Rich lavender, double in May and June, single from June to September. Flowers 6–8 in (15–20 cm). Height 6–8 ft (2–2.5 m). *Florida* group. No pruning.

'Miss Bateman'    Creamy-white overlapping sepals, medium-sized flowers which on first opening have green bars down the centre of each sepal. Chocolate-red stamens. May, June and September. Flowers 4–6 in (10–15 cm). Height 6–8 ft (2–2.5 m). *Patens* group. No pruning.

'Miss Crawshay'    Mauve-pink with pale fawn stamens, semi-double flowers in May and June. Single flowers from June to September. Flowers 4–6 in (10–15 cm). Height 6–8 ft (2–2.5 m). *Florida* group. No pruning.

'Monte Cassino'    Vivid red with creamy stamens. June to September. Flowers 4–6 in (10–15 cm). Height 6–8 ft (2–2.5 m). *Jackmanii* group. Hard pruning.

'Moonlight'    Soft primrose with yellow stamens, the nearest variety to yellow yet. Also known as 'Yellow Queen' and 'Wada's Primrose'. May, June and September. Flowers 6–8 in (10–15 cm). Height 6–8 ft (2–2.5 m). *Patens* group. No pruning.

'Mrs Bush'    Deep lavender-blue, long narrow sepals and pale brown stamens. June to September. Flowers 8–10 in (20–25 cm). Height 8–12 ft (2.5–3.5 m). *Lanuginosa* group. Pruning optional.

'Mrs Cholmondeley'    Lavender-blue with long narrow sepals and brown stamens. The longest-flowering variety of all, vigorous and free-flowering. May to September. Flowers 7–9 in (17–22 cm). Height 12–16 ft (3.5–5 m). *Lanuginosa* group. Pruning optional.

'Mrs George Jackman'    Creamy-white flowers with rounded sepals and brown stamens. Very free-flowering. June to September.

'Silver Moon'. Very free-flowering and a unique colour.

126

Flowers 6−8 in (15−20 cm). Height 6−8 ft (2−2.5 m). *Lanuginosa* group. Pruning optional.

'Mrs Hope'    Satiny light blue flowers with overlapping sepals and red stamens. June to September. Flowers 6−8 in (15−20 cm). Height 8−12 ft (2.5−3.5 m). *Lanuginosa* group. Pruning optional.

'Mrs N. Thompson'    Deep violet-blue with vivid scarlet bar, pointed sepals and deep red stamens. Very free-flowering. May, June and September. Flowers 4−6 in (10−15 cm). Height 6−8 ft (2−2.5 m). *Patens* group. No pruning.

'Mrs Oud'    Milk-white rounded overlapping sepals with dark stamens. June to August. Flowers 4−6 in (10−15 cm). Height 6−8 ft (2−2.5 m). *Lanuginosa* group. Pruning optional.

'Mrs P. B. Truax'    Periwinkle-blue with yellow stamens. May, June and September. Flowers 4−6 in (10−15 cm). Height 8−12 ft (2.5−3.5 m). *Patens* group. No pruning.

'Mrs Spencer Castle'    Heliotrope-pink with golden stamens. Double flowers in May and June, single flowers from June to September. Flowers 4−6 in (10−15 cm). Height 8−12 ft (2.5−3.5 m). *Florida* group. No pruning.

'Myojo'    Velvety violet-red with deeper bar and cream stamens. May, June and September. Flowers 4−6 in (10−15 cm). Height 6−8 ft (2−2.5 m). *Patens* group. No pruning.

'Nelly Moser'    Pale mauve-pink with deep carmine bars on each wide pointed sepal; a very popular variety. May, June and September. Flowers 7−9 in (17−22 cm). Height 6−8 ft (2−2.5 m). *Patens* group. No pruning.

'Niobe'    Deep ruby-red, the deepest clematis yet, almost black when first opening, pointed sepals and golden stamens. June to September continuously. Flowers 4−6 in (10−15 cm). Height 6−8 ft (2−2.5 m). *Jackmanii* group. Prune hard.

'Pennell's Purity'    Warm white with firm crimpy sepals, often semi-double, golden stamens. June to September. Flowers 6−8 in (15−20 cm). Height 6−8 ft (2−2.5 m). *Lanuginosa* group. Pruning optional.

'Percy Lake'    Porcelain-blue tinted pink with golden stamens. June and September. Flowers 4−6 in (10−15 cm). Height 6−8 ft (2−2.5 m). *Patens* group. No pruning.

*C. spooneri*, also known as *C. chrysocoma sericea*. Slightly later than the *montana* group.

*C. tangutica* will make a very big plant if left unpruned. If space is limited, prune hard in February.

'Percy Picton'     Rosy-purple with dark stamens, paler flowers in late summer. May, June and September. Flowers 6–8 in (15–20 cm). Height 6–8 ft (2–2.5 m). *Patens* group. No pruning.

'Percy Robinson'     Lavender-pink with golden stamens. June to September. Flowers 6–8 in (15–20 cm). Height 8–12 ft (2.5–3.5 m). *Lanuginosa* group. Pruning optional.

'Perle d'Azur'     Sky-blue with green stamens. Semi-nodding flowers with blunt-tipped corrugated sepals. Vigorous and showy. June to September continuously. Flowers 4–6 in (10–15 cm). Height 10–16 ft (3–5 m). *Jackmanii* group. Prune hard.

'Peveril Pearl'     Lustrous lilac with pink bar and cream stamens. May, June and August. Flowers 6–8 in (15–20 cm). Height 6–8 ft (2–2.5 m). *Patens* group. No pruning.

'Pink Fantasy'     Shell-pink with deeper bar and attractive twisted sepals. Very free-flowering. June to September. Flowers 4–6 in (10–15 cm). Height 6–8 ft (2–2.5 m). *Jackmanii* group. Prune hard.

'Prince Charles'     Mauve-blue medium-sized flowers, green stamens June to September. Flowers 4–6 in (10–15 cm). Height 6–8 ft (2–2.5 m). *Jackmanii* group. Hard pruning.

'Princess of Wales'     Satiny-mauve with dark stamens. June to September. Flowers 6–8 in (15–20 cm). Height 8–12 ft (2.5–3.5 m). *Patens* group. No pruning.

'Prins Hendrik'     Lavender-blue with purple stamens. Sepals large and pointed with crimped edges. June to August. Flowers 8–10 in (20–25 cm). Height 6–8 ft (2–2.5 m). *Patens* group. No pruning.

'Proteus'     Rosy-lilac with yellow stamens, semi-double in May and June, single from June to September. Flowers 6–8 in (15–20 cm). Height 6–8 ft (2–2.5 m). *Florida* group. No pruning.

'Ramona'     Lavender-blue overlapping rounded sepals with dark stamens, also known as hybrida 'Seiboldii'. June to September. Flowers 6–8 in (15–20 cm). Height 12–16 ft (3.5–5 m). *Lanuginosa* group. Pruning optional.

'Richard Pennell'     Warm rosy-purple with saucer-shaped overlapping sepals and a gold and maroon centre. Flowers 6–8 in (15–20 cm). Height 6–8 ft (2–2.5 m). *Patens* group. No pruning.

'Rouge Cardinal'     Glowing crimson with blunt-tipped recurving

*C. texensis* 'Sir Trevor Lawrence'. A very rare semi-herbaceous late-flowering variety.

*C. texensis* 'Gravetye Beauty'. This variety opens wider than the others in this group.

sepals and brown stamens, June to September continuously. Flowers 4−6 in (10−15 cm). Height 6−8 ft (2−2.5 m). *Jackmanii* group. Prune hard.

'Ruby Lady'     Ruby-red with brown stamens. June to September. Flowers 4−6 in (10−15 cm). Height 6−8 ft (2−2.5 m). *Lanuginosa* group. Pruning optional.

'Sally Cadge'     Mid-blue with carmine bars. Very free and vigorous, a cross between 'Nelly Moser' and 'Lasurstern'. May and June and again in September. Flowers 6−8 in (15−20 cm). Height 6−8 ft (2−2.5 m). *Patens* group. No pruning.

'Saturn'    Lavender-blue with maroon bar and white stamens. May, June and September. Flowers 6–8 in (15–20 cm). Height 6–8 ft (2–2.5 m). *Patens* group. No pruning.

'Scartho Gem'    Bright deep pink, vigorous and free-flowering. Golden stamens. June to September. Flowers 6–8 in (15–20 cm). Height 6–8 ft (2–2.5 m). *Lanuginosa* group. Pruning optional.

'Sealand Gem'    Rosy-mauve with a petunia bar on each wavy sepal, brown stamens. June to September. Flowers 4–6 in (10–15 cm). Height 8–12 ft (2.5–3.5 m). *Lanuginosa* group. Pruning optional.

'Serenata'    Dusky-purple sepals with darker bars and contrasting bright yellow stamens. Very free-flowering. May to September. Flowers 4–6 in (10–15 cm). Height 8–12 ft (2.5–3.5 m). *Jackmanii* group. Prune hard.

'Sho Un'    Soft lavender overlapped sepals with deep-toned veins. Beautiful white stamens. June to September. Flowers 8–10 in (20–25 cm). Height 6–8 ft (2–2.5 m). *Lanuginosa* group. Pruning optional.

'Silver Moon'    Mother of pearl grey with yellow stamens. Very free-flowering. June to September. Flowers 6–8 in (15–20 cm). Height 8–12 ft (2.5–3.5 m). *Lanuginosa* group. Pruning optional.

'Sir Garnet Wolseley'    Mauve-blue with a pale purplish bar. Reddish-purple stamens. May, June and August. Flowers 6–8 in (15–20 cm). Height 6–8 ft (2–2.5 m). *Patens* group. No pruning.

'Snow Queen'    Snow-white with pink bars in late summer. Brown stamens. May, June and September. Flowers 6–8 in (15–20 cm). Height 8–12 ft (2.5–3.5 m). *Patens* group. No pruning.

'Star of India'    Reddish-plum with a red bar. Vigorous and free-flowering. Yellow stamens. June to September continuously. Flowers 4–6 in (10–15 cm). Height 12–20 ft (3.5–6 m). *Jackmanii* group. Prune hard.

'Susan Allsop'    Rosy-purple with a red bar, magenta red centre and golden stamens. June to September. Flowers 6–8 in (15–20 cm). Height 6–8 ft (2–2.5 m). *Lanuginosa* group. Pruning optional.

'Sylvia Denny'    Double white with yellow stamens. May and June. Single in September. Flowers 4–6 in (10–15 cm). Height 6–8 ft (2–2.5 m). *Florida* group. No pruning.

'Sympathia'    Rosy-lilac with deep brown stamens. July to October.

'The President'. A very free-flowering and reliable variety.

Flowers 6−8 in (15−20 cm). Height 6−8 ft (2−2.5 m). *Lanuginosa* group. Pruning optional.

'The President'    Deep purple-blue with handsome pointed sepals and reddish-purple stamens. June to September. Flowers 6−8 in (15−20 cm). Height 6−8 ft (2−2.5 m). *Patens* group. No pruning.

'Tsuzuki'    Pure white with yellow stamens. A beautiful variety from Japan. June to September. Flowers 4−6 in (10−15 cm). Height 6−8 ft (2−2.5 m). *Lanuginosa* group. Pruning optional.

'Twilight'    Deep petunia-mauve with yellow stamens. July to October continuously. Flowers 6−8 in (15−20 cm). Height 6−8 ft (2−2.5 m). *Jackmanii* group. Prune hard.

'Venosa Violacea'    Violet-blue pencilled with white veins. Purple stamens. June to September continuously. Flowers 4−6 in (10−15 cm). Height 10−16 ft (3−5 m). *Viticella* group. Prune hard.

'Veronica's Choice'    Semi-double lavender with crimpy sepals. June to September. Flowers 6−8 in (15−20 cm). Height 8−12 ft (2.5−3.5 m). *Lanuginosa* group. Pruning optional.

'Victoria'    Soft rosy-purple with buff-coloured stamens. Vigorous and free-flowering. June to September continuously. Flowers 4−6 in (10−15 cm). Height 10−16 ft (3−5 m). *Jackmanii* group. Prune hard.

'Ville de Lyon'    Carmine red edged with deep crimson, golden stamens. Very free-flowering and vigorous. July to October continuously. Flowers 4−6 in (10−15 cm). Height 8−12 ft (2.5−3.5 m). *Jackmanii* group. Prune hard.

'Vino'    Rosy-red with attractive cream incurving stamens. May, June and September. Flowers 6−8 in (15−20 cm). Height 6−8 ft (2−2.5 m). *Patens* group. No pruning.

'Violet Charm'    Rich violet with handsome, long, pointed sepals and light brown stamens. Flowers 7−9 in (17−22 cm). Height 6−8 ft (2−2.5 m). *Lanuginosa* group. Pruning optional.

'Violet Elizabeth'    Double delicate mauve-pink. May and June. Single in September. Yellow stamens. Flowers 6−8 in (15−20 cm). Height 6−8 ft (2−2.5 m). *Florida* group. No pruning.

'Voluceau'    Petunia-red with yellow stamens. Very vigorous and free-flowering. June to September continuously. Flowers 4−6 in (10−15 cm). Height 8−12 ft (2.5−3.5 m). *Jackmanii* group. Prune hard.

'Venosa Violacea'. A good summer-flowering variety.

'Vyvyan Pennell'     Double deep violet-blue, suffused purple and red in the centre. Golden stamens. May and June. Single lavender-blue flowers in late summer and autumn. Flowers 6–8 in (15–20 cm). Height 6–8 ft (2–2.5 m). *Florida* group. No pruning.

'Wada's Primrose' see 'Moonlight'.

'Walter Pennell'     Deep pink double flowers with a mauve tinge in May and June. Single flowers in the autumn. Buff coloured stamens. Flowers 6–8 in (15–20 cm). Height 6–8 ft (2–2.5 m). *Florida* group. No pruning.

'Warszawska Nike' (pronounced neekay)     Rich royal purple with golden stamens. June to September. Flowers 6–8 in (15–20 cm). Height 8–12 ft (2.5–3.5 m). *Jackmanii* group. Prune hard.

'W. E. Gladstone'     Lilac-blue with purple stamens and large flat sepals. June to September. Flowers 8–10 in (20–25 cm). Height 8–12 ft (2.5–3.5 m). *Lanuginosa* group. Pruning optional.

'Wilhelmina Tull'     Deep violet with crimson bar and golden stamens. May, June and September. Flowers 4–6 in (10–15 cm). Height 6–8 ft (2–2.5 m). *Patens* group. No pruning.

'Will Goodwin'     Lavender-blue, deeply veined with frilled edges to sepals and golden stamens. June to September. Flowers 6–8 in (15–20 cm). Height 8–12 ft (2.5–3.5 m). *Lanuginosa* group. Pruning optional.

'William Kennett'     Deep lavender-blue with crimped overlapping pointed sepals. Dark purple stamens. Vigorous and free-flowering. June to September. Flowers 6–8 in (15–20 cm). Height 8–12 ft (2.5–3.5 m). *Lanuginosa* group. Pruning optional.

'Xerxes' ('Elsa Spath')     Deep violet-blue with purple shading, rounded overlapping sepals and reddish-purple stamens. June to September. Flowers 6–8 in (15–20 cm). Height 6–8 ft (2–2.5 m). *Lanuginosa* group.

'Yellow Queen' see 'Moonlight'.

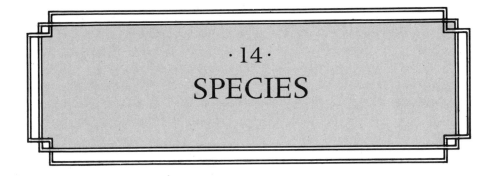

# ·14·
# SPECIES

he description of species is a little more detailed than that given for hybrids. They are much more diverse in shape and size and they come from different parts of the world. Species need little pruning and can be left to ramble at will through hedges, trees, etc., but where there are confined spaces, such as on walls, then some pruning is sometimes necessary. The early-flowering varieties such as *C. alpina, C. macropetala* and *C. montana* need no pruning but can, if necessary, be cut back directly after flowering, which will be in May or early June, thus giving them plenty of time to grow during the summer. The later-flowering varieties can be cut back hard, treating them as Jackmaniis, but here again, if space is no object, they can be left to garland gracefully everything within their reach.

*C. afoliata*    The rush-stemmed clematis grows wild in New Zealand. It is a rather untidy plant in growth with masses of rush-stemmed dark green, almost leafless, stems which turn yellow in the autumn. Clusters of small tubular-shaped pale yellow flowers appear in May, having a sweet daphne scent. Rather tender and should be grown on a south or west wall or in some sheltered spot. Will grow up to 8 ft (2.5 m) and needs no pruning.

*C. apiifolia*    Small creamy-white flowers produced in axillary panicles in August and September. Tri-foliate leaves which are deeply toothed. Needs hard pruning every winter. Grows to a height of about 10 ft (3 m).

*C. australis*    A tender species from New Zealand which requires a sheltered position in the garden, or will grow well in a conservatory. Small evergreen finely cut foliage and small greeny-white scented flowers in April and May. No pruning.

*C. alpina* (syn. 'Atragene')    The alpine virgin's bower, so called because it is found growing wild in the alpine regions of Southern Europe. These *alpina* and *macropetala* varieties were originally listed as a separate species called *Atragene*, but they are now listed under the name of *Clematis*. They have coarsely toothed leaves, with nodding satiny-blue flowers in April and May, grow to about 6–8 ft (2–2.5 m) and are ideal for north-facing walls or cool positions in the garden. They are also useful for growing on rockeries and will scramble over the rocks naturally as they do in the wild. No pruning is necessary.

*C. alpina* 'Burford White'  Clear white.
*C. alpina* 'Columbine'  Pale blue.
*C. alpina* 'Pamela Jackman'  Rich mid-blue.
*C. alpina* 'Ruby'  Rosy-red.
*C. alpina sibirica*  Creamy-white.
*C. alpina* 'White Moth'  Double white.
*C. alpina* 'Willy'  Pale pink.
(All these varieties have the same habit as *C. alpina* and need no pruning.)

*C. aristata*  The wild Australian clematis which grows in profusion around the village of Clematis in the Dandenong highland areas of Victoria, Australia. Masses of small white flowers in the spring with evergreen leaves. A vigorous variety growing to about 20 ft (6 m).

*C. armandii*  Armand's clematis. So named in honour of Père Armand David 1826–1900, a French missionary. This beautiful clematis grows wild in southern China and was introduced by E. H. Wilson in 1900. It is a plant that needs plenty of room as it will grow to 20–30 ft (6–9 m) and is one of the few evergreen clematis. The large trifoliate 6 in (15 cm) long glossy green leaves are a feature of the plant. The flowers appear in bunches at the leaf axils in April and May. They are pure white with four or six sepals and yellow stamens, and are very fragrant. This clematis is a little tender and should be grown on sheltered south-facing walls in the north, in the south it can be grown in the open and only gets cut back in very severe winters. No pruning needed.
*C. armandii* 'Apple Blossom'  A pale pink variety.
*C. armandii* 'Snowdrift'  Pure white, larger than *C. armandii*.
(Both these varieties have the same habit as *C. armandii*.)

*C. calycina* (syn. *C. balearica*)  The fern-leaved clematis, a native of the Balearic Islands in the Mediterranean. Introduced in 1783. Another evergreen clematis with slender stems and fern-like deep green foliage which turns bronzy in the winter. Although evergreen, this variety will sometimes lose its leaves in the late summer and autumn, but fresh green leaves will appear in December followed by attractive small bell-shaped pale yellow flowers with red freckles within, flowering throughout the winter until March or April. It makes quite a big plant, growing up to 20 ft (6 m) and will grow in any position. Supposed to be scented but I have never detected any,

*C. thibetanus.* A very rare variety which illustrates the great diversity of clematis flowers.

possibly if brought into a warm room its delicate fragrance would be released. No pruning.

*C. campaniflora*   The harebell clematis. A native of Portugal. A vigorous climber with divided pinnate leaves. The dainty bell-shaped, pale blue nodding flowers 1 in (2.5 cm) in diameter are produced freely in late summer. It will grow to about 10 ft (3 m). No pruning.

*C. chrysocoma*   The hairy clematis. So called as its young shoots and leaves are covered with golden brown hairy down. Allied to the *montanas* but the leaves are quite different, being softer-looking because of the down-covered foliage. The flowers are pale pink and cup-shaped and produced freely in May and June. A few flowers will also appear on the young wood in the summer. Grows to a height of about 20 ft (6 m). No pruning.

*C. cirrhosa*   Another evergreen often confused with *C. calycina*, but its foliage is of tri-lobed ovate leaves, not fern-like as with *C. calycina*. The small flowers are bell-shaped, pendulous and creamy-white with no freckles inside, and as well as flowering in the winter it will also produce flowers in the summer on young wood. A native of Southern Europe and North Africa, it will grow to a height of about 10–15 ft (3–4 m). No pruning.

*C. davidiana*      see *C. heracleifolia*

*C. douglasii* var. *scotiae*   A herbaceous variety from America with pitcher-shaped mauve-blue flowers produced in July and August amid glaucous foliage. Large fluffy seedheads in the autumn. Grows to about 2 ft (60 cm) and needs hard pruning every winter.

139

*C. eriostemon*    A semi-herbaceous plant which will grow to a height of 6—8 ft (2—2.5 m) with large simple ovate leaves. The dusky-blue flowers are of four sepals, bell-shaped and hang downwards. They are produced freely July to September. Dies down to the ground in the winter. One of the earliest varieties to be raised in England in 1820 by Mr Henderson of London and was a cross between *C. integrifolia* and *C. viticella*. Should be pruned hard during the winter.

*C. fargesii* var. *soulei*    There seem to have been a number of French missionaries in China in the nineteenth century and this variety was named after another one, Père Paul Farges, 1844—1912. It is a vigorous climber, growing up to 20 ft (6 m). The leaves are hairy and purplish-green. The flowers are pure white 2—3 in (5—7.5 cm) across, produced from June to September and resembling those of the blackberry (*Rubus* spp). Pruning optional.

*C. finetiana*    An evergreen variety which is slightly tender and needs a warm wall. It has small hawthorn-scented white flowers in June. Needs no pruning. It grows to a height of 16 ft (5 m).

*C. flammula*    The fragrant virgin's bower. A very sweetly scented variety, it will fill the garden with its hawthorn perfume on moist calm days. Thousands of small white flowers are produced in late summer and early autumn. Very vigorous, growing up to 20 ft (6 m). Will cover small trees and bushes and do no harm to its hosts. The flowers are followed by silky grey seedheads. No pruning, but if space is limited it can be pruned in the spring, as it flowers on the young wood only.

*C. flammula rubra marginata* – also called *C. triternata rubra marginata*. A cross between *C. flammula* and *C. viticella*. The tiny flowers are edged with rosy-purple and are scented. A vigorous variety. Pruning as for *C. flammula*.

*C. florida bicolor* (*sieboldii*)    A very striking, but slender, plant, introduced from Japan in 1837. The creamy-white flowers with a centre of purple petaloid stamens are produced freely from June to September and are often thought to be passion flowers. Needs a very sheltered spot in the garden but is ideal to grow in large pots or tubs in a cold greenhouse or conservatory. Grows to a height of 6—8 ft (2—2.5 m). Should be pruned back about half-way in early spring.

*C. florida alba plena*    A white variety with a double centre of white petaloid stamens. 6—8 ft (2—2.5 m).

*C. fosterii*    A New Zealand evergreen variety with small creamy-white six- to eight-sepalled flowers with a mass of attractive golden stamens in the centre and a lovely lemon verbena scent. Not hardy in Britain, but successful in a frost-free conservatory. Pruning optional.

'Victoria'. A good plant and a change from the purple 'Jackmanii'. (*right*)

'Violet Elizabeth'. An unusual double variety. (*far right*)

*C. fusca*    An unusual and rare variety with small urn-shaped brownish-purple flowers. Height 10–12 ft (3–3.5 m). Prune hard.

*C. glauca*    Bell-shaped orange flowers in August and September with glaucous, finely cut foliage, similar to *C. orientalis*. Grows to 20 ft (6 m) and can be pruned hard every winter, or left unpruned if you have plenty of room.

*C. grata*    A vigorous climber with large coarse leaves, growing to 20–30 ft (6–9 m). Ideal for rambling through trees and shrubs. Small bluish-white scented flowers appear in late summer. Pruning optional.

*C. heracleifolia* 'Cote d'Azur'    Herbaceous variety with large coarse leaves. Produces clusters of small pale blue hyacinth-like flowers from the leaf axils in August and September. Grows to about 2–3 ft (60–90 cm). Prune hard in winter.

*C. heracleifolia davidiana*    A herbaceous variety from China introduced by, and named after, the Abbé David, a French missionary, in 1864. The small hyacinth-like blue tubular-shaped flowers are produced in late summer in bunches at each leaf axil, and are sweetly scented. It is an ideal border plant as it makes a bush about 2–3 ft high (60–90 cm). It should be cut back to the base of the plant every winter.

*C. heracleifolia* 'Wyevale' produces larger flowers than the type. These are a deep hyacinth-blue and sweetly scented. Flowers in August and September. Grows to about 3 ft (90 cm). Prune hard in winter.

141

*C. integrifolia*   Another herbaceous variety which makes a small bushy plant of about 2 ft (60 cm). Ideal for the border. Produces its small bell-shaped blue flowers from June to August. A native of Southern Europe. Prune hard in the winter.

*C. integrifolia* 'Durandii'   A cross between *C. integrifolia* and C. 'Jackmanii', raised in France in 1870. It makes a plant of 6–8 ft (2–2.5 m) with large simple entire leaves which do not cling to their support, so that the plant must be tied up. The flowers are deep violet-blue with four sepals which are deeply ribbed and are produced from June to September. Pruning optional.

*C. integrifolia* 'Hendersonii'   A variety with larger bell-shaped deep blue flowers than the type. Makes a plant of about 2 ft (60 cm). Flowers from June to September. Prune hard in winter.

*C. integrifolia* 'Olgae'   A variety with clear blue twisted sepals, very sweetly scented. Grows to about 2 ft (60 cm). Flowers June to September. Prune hard in winter.

*C. integrifolia rosea*   A sugar-pink variety with the same habit as the type. Prune hard in winter.

*C. jouiniana*   A vigorous climber, its large leaves are non clinging so it has to be tied, or it can be grown through a small tree or shrub where its stems can cascade down. Also useful for covering tree stumps, etc. The flowers are small and bluish-white and produced freely from the leaf axils in late summer and early October. Will grow up to 10 ft (3 m) and more. Ideal for ground cover. Pruning optional.

*C. ladakhiana*   A star-shaped 2-in (5 cm) wide flower, old gold in colour with red freckles both inside and out. Fern-like foliage makes this a most interesting species. It flowers in August and September, growing to a height of 15 ft (4.5 m) and should be planted in a sunny position. Pruning optional.

*C. lanuginosa*   The woolly-leaved clematis. One of the original large-flowering species first brought from China to Britain in 1850 and the parent of many of our large-flowering hybrids. Large pale lilac-blue flowers 6–8 in (15–20 cm) in diameter with very prominent white stamens produced in June and July. Grows to 6–10 ft (2–3 m).

*C. macropetala* (syn. *Atragene macropetala*)   One of the most graceful of the species, this variety was discovered in China and introduced to Britain in 1910 by Reginald Farrer. Its beautiful small lavender-blue nodding flowers are produced early in the spring in great profusion. They have a double row of sepals with inner bluish-white petaloid staminodes. Also known as the downy clematis, as the young shoots are covered with down. Grows up to 10–12 ft (3–3.5 m).

*C. macropetala* 'Bluebird'   Deep blue.

*C. macropetala* 'Maidwell Hall'   Oxford blue.

*C. macropetala* 'Markhamii' also known as Markhams Pink   Lavender-pink.

*C. viticella*. The wild clematis of Spain with several of its varieties. (*above, right*)

*C. viticella* 'Abundance'. (*above, far right*)

*C. viticella rubra* (red) and *C. viticella* 'Etoile Violette' (purple) (*above, below right*)

*C. viticella* 'Little Nell'. (*above, below far right*)

*C. viticella alba luxurians* (*opposite, right*)

*C. viticella* 'Kermesina'. (*opposite, far right*)

*C. viticella* 'Minuet'. (*below, right*)

*C. viticella* 'Royal Velours'. (*below, far right*)

143

*C. macropetala* 'Rosy O'Grady'      Pink with long pointed sepals.

*C. macropetala* 'Snowbird'      Pure white, later flowering.

*C. macropetala* 'White Swan'      Snow-white.

(All these varieties have the same habit as *C. macropetala* and need no pruning.)

*C. maximowicziana*      The sweet autumn clematis of America. Previously know as *C. paniculata* which is now known as *C. indivisa*! (How confusing can you get, let's hope the International Clematis Society will sort things out.) Poor *maximowicziana* is a very late bloomer with masses of hawthorn-scented white flowers in September and October, but only if there is a hot summer! It grows to a height of 20–30 ft (6–9 m). Can be left unpruned or pruned hard in February if there is little room.

*C. montana*      The great Indian virgin's bower was introduced to Britain by Countess Amherst in 1831 and it is well known, in its white and pink forms, for its marvellous displays in May and June. The flowers are four-sepalled, about 2 in (5 cm) across. Some are sweetly scented and thousands of them cover a well-grown plant which will grow to 20–30 ft (6–9 m) and more. They are ideal for covering pergolas, sheds, garages and trees, and where there is plenty of room there is no need to prune. If space is limited they can be pruned hard directly after flowering, which will be late June or early July. This gives the plant plenty of time to make enough wood during the rest of the summer. This will be flowering wood for the following spring, so no flowering season is missed.

*C. montana* 'Alexander'      Creamy-white flowers with yellow stamens, scented.

*C. montana* 'Broughton Star'      Semi-double deep pink flowers with golden stamens.

*C. montana* 'Elizabeth'      Pale pink with yellow stamens, very sweetly scented.

*C. montana* 'Freda'      Cherry-pink with darker edges and golden stamens, bronzy foliage, less vigorous.

*C. montana grandiflora*      Pure white with yellow stamens.

*C. montana* 'Marjorie'      Semi-double creamy-pink sepals with salmony-pink petaloid stamens.

*C. montana* 'Mayleen'      Deep pink large flowers with golden stamens and attractive bronzy foliage.

*C. montana* 'Pink Perfection'      Good pink with yellow stamens, very vigorous and free-flowering.

*C. montana rubens*      Deep pink small flowers, golden stamens and bronzy foliage, less vigorous.

*C. montana rubens* 'Pictons Variety'      Satiny-pink flowers often with five or six sepals.

*C. montana tetrarose*      The largest flower in the *montana* range. Lilac-rose with straw-coloured stamens. A shorter flowering period than other varieties, however.

Brother Stefan Franczak has raised several new clematis in the garden of a monastery in Warsaw, Poland. Here he is seen with one of his new varieties, 'Matka Teresa' (Mother Teresa).

A few of the clematis Brother Franczak has introduced and registered with the International Clematis Society: (a) 'Ada Sari'; (b) 'Fryderyk Chopin'; (c) 'Jan Pawel II' (John Paul II); (d) 'Kacper'; (e) 'Monte Cassino'.

*C. montana* 'Wilsonii'    Creamy-white twisted sepals with prominent yellow stamens. Strongly scent resembling hot chocolate.
(All the above varieties have the same habit as *C. montana* and need no pruning.)

*C. napaulensis* (syn. *C. forestii*)    A rare winter-flowering semi-evergreen species. The flowers are long, narrow, drooping and creamy-yellow, with prominent purple stamens. Not very hardy except in south-west districts of the British Isles but useful in a cool greenhouse. Grows to a height of 20 ft (6 m). Pruning optional.

*C. orientalis* syn. *graveolens*    An attractive variety from Tibet with finely cut foliage and a profusion of nodding orange flowers with brown stamens 1–2 in (2–5 cm) in diameter. These are four-sepalled and before opening they resemble a small orange, which, with the colour and thickness of the sepals when open, gives them the popular name of the orange peel clematis. It will grow to a height of 20 ft (6 m), flowers from July to October and can be left unpruned if you have plenty of room, or pruned hard in the winter if space is limited. The flowers, which start at the base of the plant, soon turn into attractive seedheads, so that, with new flowers appearing further up the plant as the season progresses, one has flowers and seedheads all at the same time.
*C. orientalis* 'Bill MacKenzie'    The largest flowers in the *orientalis* group.
*C. orientalis* 'Burford Variety'    Very vigorous and free-flowering, but the flowers do not open so widely as the type, and thus resemble small oranges.
*C. orientalis* 'Corry'    Lemon-coloured flowers.
*C. orientalis* 'L & S 13342'    A species from Tibet with very finely cut foliage. Introduced by Ludlow and Sherriff in 1947 but why they never gave it a name I have no idea. It is the best of the *orientalis* varieties. Not quite so vigorous.
(All the above varieties have the same habit and the same colour of flowers.) Pruning is optional.

*C. paniculata* (originally known as *indivisa lobata*, see also *C. maximowicziana*)    An introduction from New Zealand, this needs a sheltered position or will grow well in a conservatory. Six to eight pure white sepals with pink stamens. Evergreen with leathery foliage. Flowers in May and June, grows to about 10–15 ft (3–5 m) and needs no pruning.

*C. pitcheri*    Urn-shaped solitary violet-purple flowers 2 in (5 cm) long with recurving tips. Flowers July to September. Dies back a little to the ground in the winter. Grows to a height of about 10 ft (3 m).

*C. recta*    The white herbaceous virgin's bower. Another excellent herbaceous variety with tall stems 3–4 ft (1–1.5 m) with glabrous

146

'Ernest Markham'.
Named after William
Robinson's gardener
at Gravetye Manor
in Sussex.

pinnate leaves and, at the top of the stems, panicles of small white flowers which are sweetly scented. Makes a handsome bush. Prune down to the base every winter.

*C. recta purpurea*   The young shoots of this variety are purple-bronze in colour but otherwise the same as *C. recta*.

*C. rehderiana*   The nodding virgin's bower (syn. *C. nutans*). Vigorous and untidy habit with coarsely toothed leaves but very attractive small flowers which are primrose-yellow, tubular-shaped, nodding and with recurving tips. To add to this it has a heavenly cowslip scent. It flowers from August to October. It will grow to a height of 10–20 ft (3–6 m). Can be left unpruned if there is plenty of room or can be pruned hard in the winter if space is limited. Ideal for scrambling through trees and shrubs but choose a south-facing aspect as late varieties need the full sun.

*C. serratifolia*   The cut-leaf clematis. Introduced from Korea in 1918. Small pale yellow flowers with sepals wide open revealing red stamens to make an attractive contrast. Very free-flowering from August to October, followed by fluffy seedheads. A vigorous variety growing 10–12 ft (3–3.5 m). Ideal for sunny walls, which all late-flowering varieties prefer. Can be pruned hard every year as it has all the year in which to grow and make flowering wood for the autumn.

*C. spooneri* (syn. *C. chrysocoma sericea*)   Similar to the *montanas*, this variety has pure white flowers, larger than the *montanas*, with golden stamens. A very free-flowering variety which lasts for several weeks. Excellent for covering trees, garages, walls etc., and will grow to 20–30 ft (6–9 m). No pruning.

*C. spooneri rosea* Apple-blossom-pink with winged sepals and the same habit as *spooneri*.

*C. tangutica* 'Gravetye' The Russian virgin's bower. Masses of deep yellow lantern-shaped small flowers with brown stamens. The early flowers quickly develop into attractive silky seedheads which mingle unusually with the later flowers. Very vigorous and free-flowering. Grows to a height of 15–20 ft (5–6 m). Can be pruned in the winter or left unpruned.
*C. tangutica* 'Lambton Park' Yellow nodding flowers, much larger than the type. Attractive large seedheads in autumn. Pruning optional.

*C. texensis* (syn. *C. coccinea*) The scarlet clematis leather flower. A very rare variety growing wild in a few places in Texas, USA. Was introduced in 1876 but is still very difficult to obtain in Britain. The popular name tells the colour of these peculiar flowers, which are small and shaped like an urn or pitcher. The sepals are also leathery. The colour is scarlet or blood red and the plant grows to about 10 ft (3 m). It flowers from July to September, is herbaceous and dies down to the ground every winter. The following varieties are obtainable in Britain and they are, as Barry Fretwell describes in his catalogue, 'the aristocrats amongst clematis!' He says, 'Their exquisite shape and vibrant colouring could well make one believe that they "must be difficult" – whereas they are amongst the most trouble free.'
*C. texensis* 'Countess of Onslow' Medium-sized bell-shaped pink flowers with a deeper bar of colour on each sepal.
*C. texensis* 'Duchess of Albany' Deep pink bell-shaped flowers with a cherry-red bar down the centre of each sepal.
*C. texensis* 'Etoile Rose' Quite the most charming of *texensis* varieties. Bell-shaped and cerise-pink, with the sepals edged in silver.
*C. texensis* 'Gravetye Beauty' Crimson bell-shaped flowers which open wider than the other varieties.
*C. texensis* 'Pagoda' Pale pink-mauve nodding flowers which have recurring tips to the sepals.
*C. texensis* 'Sir Trevor Lawrence' Deep carmine, urn-shaped flowers. All the *texensis* varieties grow to about 10 ft (3 m) and flower from June to September. As they are semi-herbaceous they die down to the ground every winter, or should be pruned hard in February.

*C. thibetianus* Attractive nodding lime-green flowers with glaucous-green foliage. Grows to a height of about 10 ft (3 m) and flowers from July until September. Pruning optional.

*C. triternata rubra marginata* See *C. flammula rubra marginata*.

*C. vedrariensis* 'Hidcote Variety' A species of the *montana* group with deep pink flowers 2 in (5 cm) in diameter. Grows to a height of 20 ft (3 m) and flowers in May and June. No pruning.

Clematis like company. Here the rare pink *C. texensis* 'Etoile Rose' is growing happily with several other plants.

A magnificent display of 'Perle d'Azur' which flowers nonstop from June until October.

*C. vedrariensis* 'Highdown'    A cross between *C. chrysocoma* and *C. montana rubens*. A good pink with quite large flowers 2–3 in (5–7.5 cm) in diameter. Grows to 20 ft (6 m) and flowers in May and June. No pruning.

*C. viorna*    A species from the USA with small globular flowers of very thick fleshy-pink sepals. Grows to 8–10 ft (2.5–3 m) and flowers in July and August. Dies down to the ground in winter.

*C. vitalba*    Old man's beard or traveller's joy, the native clematis of Britain. The flowers are small, greenish-white and appear in August, followed by masses of feathery seedheads which clothe many trees and hedges in chalky areas in the autumn. Not suitable for small gardens as it will rampage all over the place, although it can be controlled by hard pruning, but ideal for woodlands and wild gardens where it can ramble at will for 30 ft (9 m) or more.

*C. viticella*    The purple virgin's bower, or vine bower. This clematis, native to Spain, was introduced in 1569 during the reign of Queen Elizabeth I which is one explanation for the popular name of clematis as the virgin's bower. Masses of small purple saucer-shaped flowers which hang downwards from July to October. Vigorous and will climb to 10–20 ft (3–6 m) or more. Can be pruned hard in February if necessary, but best left to clamber through trees, shrubs, etc.
*C. viticella* 'Abundance'    Light wine-red with deep red veins.
*C. viticella alba luxurians*    Creamy-white with green-tipped sepals.
*C. viticella* 'Betty Corning'    Lavender-mauve bell-shaped flowers.
*C. viticella* 'Elvan'    Purple with a cream feathered band down each sepal.
*C. viticella* 'Kermesina'    Bright red.
*C. viticella* 'Little Nell'    White shading to pale mauve at the margins.
*C. viticella* 'Mary Rose'    A very old variety which was mentioned by Parkinson in 1629. It was rediscovered growing in the garden of a manor house in Devon at the same time as King Henry VIII's flagship the *Mary Rose* was brought to the surface of the Solent in 1982 and so was named after the ship. The flowers are spiky, small and smoky-amethyst in colour and very free-flowering.
*C. viticella* 'Minuet'    Cream with the sepals edged with mauve and held on long stems.
*C. purpurea plena elegans*    Very double violet-purple.
*C. viticella* 'Royal Velours'    Deep velvety-purple.
*C. viticella rubra*    Crimson
(All these varieties have the same habit as *C. viticella* and can be pruned hard in the spring if space is limited, or left unpruned if you have room for them to ramble.)

An amusing but very true article by Ted Phillips appeared in a May 1984 issue of 'Popular Gardening' and part of it is reproduced here by kind permission of the Editor.

## The Odd Clematis

Suppose, in one of those crash quizzes, someone were to stop me and enquire, 'As a God-fearing gardener and qualified factotum, what do you consider the most spectacular, cussed, fascinating, frustrating, delightful, mutinous, enigmatic and pig-headed garden plant?' I would look my inquisitor straight between the ears and say, 'Clematis!'

Clematis, as spectacular wall scramblers, eyesore-hiders, dignified easy-on-the-eye short climbers, or simply trowelled dollops of blossom, can be worthy sights second to none. I've found room for a representative collection that isn't bad for a small garden and I wouldn't be without any of them. A few of my crew obey the laws of herbaceous plants – *Clematis integrifolia, recta, heracleifolia*. A few more are the small flowering climbing species – *C. montana, flammula, calycina, orientalis, macropetala*. But the rest are those cranky large flowering hybrids that are the burden of my opening remarks.

Most of the species have reasonably extended flowering seasons. They are reliable, they climb and they clothe and are no trouble. You can prune them to keep them within bounds or you can let them go.

*C. orientalis*, with its thick yellow sepals, gives a bonus of ornamental seedheads, as do most clematis. These put me in mind of the Beatle haircuts of the sixties, as do those of *C. macropetala* which obscures a bedroom window every spring, but its starry-blue flowers are worth any inconvenience. I've got *C. flammula* beating up an old rose-arch. It provides late interest after the roses have gone over and is strongly scented.

Now for the frustrating hybrids. From the start experts advise that these should be planted deeper than the existing soil-mark. If, or when, top growth fails, there could then be fresh shoots from the base. Clematis of this sort are vulnerable from the cradle. Quite apart from the normal pests, competition, and the weather, there are still perils to threaten top growth enough to keep you awake at nights. Wilt may get it, or it might pine away for no reason you can discover. But as your plant matures – there IS a silver lining – chances of continued survival are in direct proportion to the diameter of the stem. Even so, the dormant clematis often look dead when they aren't. They do this on purpose just to get you nervous. Much of my stock starts to break about January, but there is always the odd one that won't stir itself until weeks after. When it does open an eye, 'tis with a wink that says, plain as plain, 'nearly had you there, old fruit!'

Clematis are no respecters of class or station. I had a neighbour once who scuffed-out a shallow depression with an old shovel and planted a 'Countess of Lovelace'. He confirmed that he had been taken in by the pretty picture in the catalogue. There it performed annually, prolifically and eye-catching, with flowers now single, and anon, double. But this annoyed him. He thought he'd got an inferior plant and always grizzled because the colour didn't look at all like the picture in the catalogue. I pointed out to him that life rarely does come up to the picture in the book, and clematis are notorious in this respect anyway, especially the blues and reds. Really, he should have been consoling *me*. I spent an hour with that same 'Countess', I took 20 minutes to get the hole right before cushioning her on fibrous compost liberally laced with bonemeal, finishing off with a mulch of peat and a bonus of Growmore – and she *still* crossed the Great Divide after one winter. On the other side of the ledger, I planted a 'Duchess of Edinburgh', which many scribes have noted as notoriously dodgy, against a dry, east-facing wall, subsequently enjoying its double white flowers in quantities sufficient to make your eyes stand out like rudbeckia cones! Though after writing this eulogy I note that she looks poorly and is not so hot this year. An important lesson to learn here – never boast about them, they might get to hear about it and start acting up. When planting, I don't advocate my late neighbour's coal shovel touch, nor do I recommend the antics of folk who play music to get them going. You might take in roses or dahlias or summer bedding plants with such nonsense, but you won't fool clematis. But an alternative is to mention within the plant's hearing that you'll *try* it here. The spot doesn't look too good, but it will just have to lump it and take its chance. You then adopt classic planting procedures. Nice big hole to commiserate with its existing roots, plenty of good compost, touch of bonemeal, roots spread out, compost firmed with your fingers, main stem planted below the original Plimsoll line as already suggested, all the time stressing aloud that the thing might possibly hold the fort until you can get your hands on a decent climber. This gets it keen. You try it and see. It will shin up its support and start to wave about before you get a chance to tie it in.

Ah yes, She is indeed the Queen of Climbers. Apart from these odd minor points I won't hear a word against them.

151

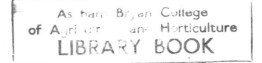

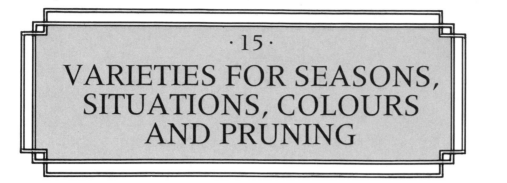

# VARIETIES FOR SEASONS, SITUATIONS, COLOURS AND PRUNING

In this chapter I have listed the best of the many varieties for flowering at the various seasons of the year. The varieties in this chapter are well known and reliable, provided they are well looked after. Detailed information for each variety will be found in chapters 13 and 14. Here I have just stated the colour to give a quick guide. For instance you can quickly select a pink variety for early spring, a red variety for the summer and a purple variety for the autumn. So in this way, by choosing one or two varieties from each section, you can have flowers for three-quarters of the year. I have also listed varieties suitable for various situations; for north walls, to grow in trees, in tubs for small gardens, doubles, in colours and for pruning.

Clematis grown on raised Netlon stretched flat across stakes so that one looks down on the flowers.

*Early spring varieties (March and April)*

| | | | |
|---|---|---|---|
| C. alpina | blue | C. calycina | pale yellow evergreen |
| C. alpina 'Columbine' | pale blue | C. cirrhosa | white evergreen |
| C. alpina 'Ruby' | ruby-red | C. macropetala | double powder-blue |
| C. alpina 'White Moth' | double white | C. macropetala 'Maidwell Hall' | double deep blue |
| C. armandii | white evergreen | C. macropetala 'Markhamii' | double pink |

*Late spring and early summer varieties (May and June)*

| | | | |
|---|---|---|---|
| 'Alice Fisk' | wisteria-blue | 'Marcel Moser' | petunia-mauve, carmine bar |
| 'Barbara Dibley' | pansy-violet | | |
| 'Barbara Jackman' | mauve with crimson bar | 'Miss Bateman' | white |
| 'Bees Jubilee' | mauve-pink, carmine bars | C. montana 'Elizabeth' | small pink, scented |
| | | C. montana 'Freda' | small cherry-pink |
| 'Capitan Thuilleaux' | strawberry-pink bars, cream edges | C. montana grandiflora | small white |
| | | C. montana 'Marjorie' | small double creamy-pink |
| 'Carnaby' | raspberry-pink | | |
| 'Corona' | pinky-purple | C. montana 'Mayleen' | small deep pink, scented |
| 'Countess of Lovelace' | double blue | | |
| 'Daniel Deronda' | double deep blue | C. montana 'Pink Perfection' | small clear pink |
| 'Dr Ruppel' | mauve-pink, deep carmine bars | C. montana rubens | small deep pink |
| | | C. montana tetrarose | slightly larger lilac-pink |
| 'Duchess of Edinburgh' | double white | C. montana 'Wilsonii' | small cream, scented |
| 'Haku Ookan' | semi-double purple | 'Mrs N. Thompson' | violet, crimson bar |
| 'H. F. Young' | blue | 'Mrs Spencer Castle' | double heliotrope |
| 'Kathleen Dunford' | semi-double, rosy-purple | 'Nelly Moser' | pale mauve-pink, carmine bar |
| 'Lasurstern' | blue | | |
| 'Lincoln Star' | raspberry-pink | 'Snow Queen' | white |
| 'Louise Rowe' | double mauve | 'Sylvia Denny' | double white |
| | | C. spooneri | small white |
| | | 'The President' | purple |
| | | 'Vyvyan Pennell' | double cerise-purple |

*Summer varieties (June to September)*

| | | | |
|---|---|---|---|
| 'Belle Nantaise' | blue | 'Lord Nevill' | rich blue |
| 'Comtesse de Bouchaud' (p) | mauve-pink | 'Madame Edouard André' (p) | wine-red |
| C. eriostemon | nodding purple | 'Madame Julia Correvon' (p) | small wine-red |
| 'Edith' | white | 'Marie Boisellot' | white |
| 'Etoile Violette' (p) | purple | 'Margot Koster' (p) | mauve-pink |
| 'General Sikorski' | blue | 'Margaret Hunt' (p) | dusky-pink |
| 'Hagley Hybrid' (p) | pink | 'Mrs Cholmondeley' | lavender-blue |
| 'Henryi' | white | 'Niobe' (p) | ruby-red |
| C. integrifolia (p) | blue herbaceous variety | C. orientalis | small orange |
| | | 'Perle d'Azur' (p) | sky-blue |
| C. integrifolia 'Durandii' | deep blue | 'Rouge Cardinal' (p) | crimson-red |
| 'Jackmanii' (p) | purple | 'Silver Moon' | pearly-grey |
| 'Jackmanii Rubra' (p) | petunia-red | C. tangutica 'Gravetye' | small yellow |
| 'Joan Picton' | lilac-pink | 'Twilight' (p) | petunia-mauve |
| 'John Huxtable' (p) | white | 'Venosa Violacea' (p) | violet |
| 'Jan Pawel II' (John Paul II) | cream | 'Victoria' (p) | heliotrope |
| 'Kathleen Wheeler' | plummy-mauve | 'Violet Charm' | violet-blue |
| 'Lady Caroline Nevill' | lavender-blue | 'Voluceau' (p) | petunia-red |
| 'Lady Northcliffe' | lavender-blue | 'W. E. Gladstone' | lilac-blue |
| 'Lawsoniana' | rosy-lavender | 'William Kennett' | lavender-blue |
| 'Lilacina Floribunda' | purple | 'Xerxes' | violet-blue |

(p) varieties needing hard pruning each year

*Late summer and autumn varieties (August to October)*

| | | | |
|---|---|---|---|
| C. campaniflora | small blue | C. texensis 'Duchess of Albany' (p) | small pink, semi-herbaceous |
| C. davidiana (p) | blue, herbaceous, scented | C. texensis 'Etoile Rose' (p) | small silvery-pink, semi-herbaceous |
| C. davidiana 'Wyevale' (p) | small blue, herbaceous, scented | C. texensis 'Gravetye Beauty' (p) | small bright red, semi-herbaceous |
| 'Ernest Markham' (p) | petunia-red | 'Ville de Lyon' (p) | carmine red |
| C. fargesii | small white | C. viticella | small purple |
| C. flammula | small white, scented | C. viticella alba luxurians | small white |
| 'Gipsy Queen' (p) | royal purple | C. viticella 'kermesina' | red |
| 'Huldine' (p) | pearly-white | C. viticella 'Minuet' | small cream, edged purple |
| C. jouiniana | small pale-blue | | |
| 'Lady Betty Balfour' (p) | blue | C. viticella purpurea plena elegans | double purple |
| C. maximowicziana | small white | | |
| C. recta (p) | small white, herbaceous, scented | C. viticella 'Royal Velour' | royal purple |
| C. rehderiana | small yellow, scented | C. viticella rubra | small crimson |

(p) varieties needing *hard pruning*

*Varieties for growing on north walls*

| | | | |
|---|---|---|---|
| C. alpina and its varieties | 'Dr Ruppel' | C. macropetala varieties | 'Silver Moon' |
| 'Alice Fisk' | 'General Sikorski' | 'Marcel Moser' | 'Snow Queen' |
| 'Barbara Dibley' | 'Hagley Hybrid' | 'Marie Boisellot' | 'The President' |
| 'Barbara Jackman' | 'H. F. Young' | 'Miss Bateman' | 'Vyvyan Pennell' |
| 'Bees Jubilee' | 'Jackmanii' | 'Mrs Cholmondeley' | 'Wada's Primrose' |
| 'Capitan Thuilleaux' | 'Jan Pawel II' (John Paul II) | C. montana varieties | 'W. E. Gladstone' |
| 'Comtesse de Bouchaud' | 'Lincoln Star' | 'Perle d'Azur' | 'Will Goodwin' |
| | 'Louise Rowe' | | 'William Kennett' |

(Descriptions will be found on pages 112–150.)

*Varieties for tubs*

| | | | |
|---|---|---|---|
| C. alpina and its varieties | 'Duchess of Edinburgh' | 'John Warren' | 'Nelly Moser' |
| 'Alice Fisk' | 'General Sikorski' | 'Kathleen Dunford' | 'Pink Fantasy' |
| 'Barbara Dibley' | 'Hagley Hybrid' | 'Lincoln Star' | 'Prince Charles' |
| 'Barbara Jackman' | 'Haku Ookan' | 'Lord Nevill' | 'Rouge Cardinal' |
| 'Beauty of Worcester' | 'H. F. Young' | 'Louise Rowe' | 'Snow Queen' |
| 'Capitan Thuilleaux' | 'Jackmanii' | C. macropetala varieties | 'The President' |
| 'Comtesse de Bouchaud' | 'Joan Picton' | 'Madame Edouard André' | 'W. E. Gladstone' |
| 'Daniel Deronda' | | 'Miss Bateman' | 'William Kennett' |
| 'Dr Ruppel' | | 'Mrs N. Thompson' | |

(Descriptions will be found on pages 112–150.)

*Varieties for growing through trees and shrubs*

| | | | |
|---|---|---|---|
| 'Bees Jubilee' | 'Henryi' | 'Margaret Hunt' | 'Ramona' |
| 'Comtesse de Bouchaud' | 'H. F. Young' | C. maximowicziana | C. serratifolia |
| 'Duchess of Edinburgh' | 'Huldine' | C. montana varieties | C. spooneri |
| 'Ernest Markham' | 'Jackmanii' | 'Mrs Cholmondeley' | 'Star of India' |
| 'Etoile Violette' | 'Lawsoniana' | 'Mrs Spencer Castle' | C. viticella varieties |
| C. flammula | 'Madame Baron Veillard' | C. orientalis | 'Ville de Lyon' |
| 'Gipsy Queen' | | 'Perle d'Azur' | 'William Kennett' |

(Descriptions will be found on pages 112–150.)

*Varieties for small gardens*

| | | | |
|---|---|---|---|
| *C. alpina* varieties | 'Dr Ruppel' | 'Kacper' | 'Niobe' |
| 'Alice Fisk' | 'Duchess of Edinburgh' | 'Lady Northcliffe' | 'Prince Charles' |
| 'Barbara Dibley' | 'Fair Rosamond' | 'Louise Rowe' | 'Rouge Cardinal' |
| 'Beauty of Worcester' | 'Hagley Hybrid' | 'Madame Edouard André' | *C. texensis* 'Gravetye |
| 'Comtesse de Bouchaud' | | 'Margot Koster' | Beauty' |
| 'Daniel Deronda' | 'Joan Picton' | 'Miss Bateman' | 'Violet Charm' |
| | 'John Warren' | | 'Xerxes' |

(Descriptions will be found on pages 112–150.)

*Hybrid varieties in their colours*

### Blue

| | | | |
|---|---|---|---|
| 'Ascotiensis' | 'Blue Diamond' | 'General Sikorski' | 'Lasurstern' |
| 'Beauty of Richmond' | 'Chalcedony' | 'H. F. Young' | 'Mrs P. B. Truax' |
| 'Beauty of Worcester' | 'Countess of Lovelace' | 'Lady Betty Balfour' | 'Perle d'Azur' |
| 'Belle Nantaise' | 'Daniel Deronda' | 'Lady Northcliffe' | 'Prince Charles' |

### Lavender Mauve

| | | | |
|---|---|---|---|
| 'Belle of Woking' | 'Lady Londesborough' | 'Princess of Wales' | 'Veronica's Choice' |
| 'Blue Gem' | 'Louise Rowe' | 'Prins Hendrik' | 'Victoria' |
| 'Bracebridge Star' | 'Miriam Markham' | 'Ramona' | 'W. E. Gladstone' |
| 'Four Star' | 'Mrs Hope' | 'Silver Moon' | 'Will Goodwin' |
| 'Lady C. Nevill' | 'Mrs Bush' | 'Sympathia' | 'William Kennett' |
| | 'Mrs Cholmondeley' | | |

### Petunia-red

| | | | |
|---|---|---|---|
| 'Barbara Dibley' | 'Keith Richardson' | 'Ruby Lady' | 'Voluceau' |
| 'Corona' | 'Ruby Glow' | 'Twilight' | |

### Pink

| | | | |
|---|---|---|---|
| 'Carnaby' | 'Elizabeth Foster' | 'Lucey' | 'Miss Crawshay' |
| 'Charissima' | 'Gladys Picard' | 'Madame Baron Veillard' | 'Pink Fantasy' |
| 'Comtesse de Bouchaud' | 'Hagley Hybrid' | 'Margaret Hunt' | 'Proteus' |
| 'Dawn' | 'John Warren' | 'Margot Koster' | 'Vino' |
| | 'Joan Picton' | | |

### Purple

| | | | |
|---|---|---|---|
| 'Corona' | 'Guiding Star' | 'John Gudmunsonn' | 'Percy Picton' |
| 'Etoile Violette' | 'Haku Ookan' | 'Kathleen Dunford' | 'Serenata' |
| 'Gipsy Queen' | 'Hidcote Purple' | 'Lilacina Floribunda' | 'The President' |
| | 'Horn of Plenty' | 'Madame Grange' | 'Venosa Violacea' |
| | 'Jackmanii' | | 'Warsaw Nike' |
| | 'Jackmanii Superba' | | 'Xerxes' |

### Wine-red

| | | | |
|---|---|---|---|
| 'Asao' | 'Jackmanii Rubra' | 'Madame Edouard André' | 'Rouge Cardinal' |
| 'Crimson King' | 'Kardynal Wyszynski' | 'Madame Julia Correvon' | 'Ville de Lyon' |
| 'Duchess of Sutherland' | | 'Niobe' | |

### Violet

| | | | |
|---|---|---|---|
| 'Edouard Desfosse' | 'Kathleen Wheeler' | 'Lord Nevill' | 'Sir Garnet Wolsey' |
| 'Etoile de Paris' | 'King Edward VII' | 'Maureen' | 'Violet Charm' |
| 'Kacper' | 'Lawsoniana' | 'Richard Pennell' | 'Vyvyan Pennell' |

## White

| | | | |
|---|---|---|---|
| 'Edith' | 'Henryi' | 'John Huxtable' | 'Mrs G. Jackman' |
| 'Ena' | 'Huldine' | 'Jan Pawel II' (John Paul II) | 'Mrs Oud' |
| 'Gillian Blades' | 'Jackmanii Alba' | 'Marie Boisellot' | 'Pennell's Purity' |
| 'Halina Noll' | 'James Mason' | 'Miss Bateman' | 'Snow Queen' |

## Yellow

| | |
|---|---|
| 'Paten's Yellow' | 'Moonlight' |

## Two Coloured Striped

| | | | |
|---|---|---|---|
| 'Bees Jubilee' | 'Fairy Queen' | 'Marcel Moser' | 'Sally Cadge' |
| 'Capitan Thuilleaux' | 'John Gudmunson' | 'Mrs N. Thompson' | 'Star of India' |
| 'Dr Ruppel' | 'King George V' | 'Myojo' | 'Susan Allsop' |
| 'Fair Rosamond' | 'Lincoln Star' | 'Nelly Moser' | 'Wilhelmina Tull' |

(Descriptions will be found on pages 112–136.)

*Species varieties in their colours*

## Blue

| | | | |
|---|---|---|---|
| *alpina* | *douglasii* var. *scotiae* | *integrifolia* 'Durandii' | *macropetala* |
| *alpina* 'Frances Rivis' | *eriostemon* | *integrifolia* 'Hendersonii' | *macropetala* 'Blue Bird' |
| *alpina* 'Columbine' | *grata* | *integrifolia* 'Olgae' | *macropetala* 'Maidwell Hall' |
| *alpina* 'Pamela Jackman' | *integrifolia* | *lanuginosa* | *viticella* 'Betty Corning' |
| *davidiana* | | | |

## Pink

| | | | |
|---|---|---|---|
| *alpina* 'Willy' | *montana* 'Broughton Star' | *montana rubens* | *texensis* 'Duchess of Albany' |
| *armandii* 'Apple Blossom' | | *montana rubens* 'Picton's Variety' | |
| *chrysocoma* | *montana* 'Elizabeth' | | *texensis* 'Etoile Rose' |
| *integrifolia rosea* | *montana* 'Pink Perfection' | *montana tetrarose* | *vedrariensis* 'Hidcote' |
| *macropetala* 'Markhamii' | *montana* 'Marjorie' | *spooneri rosea* | *vedrariensis* 'Highdown' |
| *macropetala* 'Rosy O'Grady' | *montana* 'Mayleen' | *texensis* 'Countess of Onslow' | |

## Purple

| | | | |
|---|---|---|---|
| *fusca* | *viticella* | *viticella* 'Elvan' | *viticella* 'Royal Velour' |
| *pitcheri* | *viticella* 'Little Nell' | *viticella* 'Mary Rose' | |
| *recta purpurea* | | *viticella purpurea plena elegans* | |

## Ruby-red

| | | | |
|---|---|---|---|
| *alpina* 'Ruby' | *montana* 'Mayleen' | *texensis* (*coccinea*) | *viticella* 'Abundance' |
| *flammula rubra marginata* | *montana rubens* | *texensis* 'Gravetye Beauty' | *viticella* 'Kermesina' |
| *montana* 'Freda' | | *texensis* 'Sir Trevor Lawrence' | *viticella rubra* |

## Yellow

| | | | |
|---|---|---|---|
| *afoliata* | *ladakhiana* | *orientalis* 'Bill McKenzie' | *serratifolia* |
| *calycina* | *napaulensis* | *orientalis* 'Burfordii' | *tangutica* 'Gravetye' |
| *glauca* | | *orientalis* 'Corry' | *tangutica* 'Lambton Park' |

## White

| | | | |
|---|---|---|---|
| *alpina* 'Burford White' | *cirrhosa* | *jouiaiana* | *montana* 'Wilsonii' |
| *alpina sibirica* | *fargesii soulei* | *macropetala* 'Snowbird' | *paniculata* |
| *alpina* 'White Moth' | *finetiana* | *macropetala* 'White Swan' | *recta* |
| *apiifolia* | *flammula* | *maximowicziana* | *vitalba* |
| *armandii* | *florida bicolor* | *montana* 'Alexander' | *vitalba alba luxurians* |
| *armandii* 'Snowdrift' | *florida alba* | *montana grandiflora* | *viticella* 'Minuet' |
| *australis* | *fosterii* | *montana odorata* | |

(Descriptions will be found on pages 137–150.)

### *Double varieties*

| | | | |
|---|---|---|---|
| 'Beauty of Worcester' | *C. florida alba plena* | *C. montana* 'Broughton Star' | 'Violet Elizabeth' |
| 'Belle of Woking' | 'Halina Noll' | *C. montana* 'Marjorie' | *C. viticella purpurea* |
| 'Countess of Lovelace' | | 'Mrs Spencer Castle' | *plena elegans* |
| 'Daniel Deronda' | 'Kathleen Dunford' | 'Pennell's Purity' | 'Vyvyan Pennell' |
| 'Duchess of Edinburgh' | *C. macropetala* and varieties | 'Proteus' | 'Walter Pennell' |
| *C. florida bicolor* | 'Miss Crawshay' | 'Sylvia Denny' | |

(Descriptions will be found on pages 112–150.)

# INDEX

*Note:* The page numbers of illustrations are in *italics*.